EDUCATION: Planning and Human Development

EDUCATION

Planning and Human Development

(In 8 Volumes)

Issues and Trends in Educational and Vocational Guidance

(Volume 5)

V.C. PANDEY

ISHA BOOKS
DELHI—110 033

EDUCATION: Planning and Human Development
(Education)

Rs. 7000 (Set in 8 Vols.)

ISBN: 81-8205-006-5 (Set)
ISBN: 81-8205-011-1 (Vol. 5)

Published in 2003 in India by
Isha Books, D-43, Prithviraj Road
Adarsh Nagar, Delhi-110 033

Lasertypesetting by: Varsha Graphics, Delhi
Printed at: Chawla Offset Press, Delhi

Preface

Vocational education is an integral component of lifelong learning and has a crucial role to play in this new era as an effective tool to realise the objectives of a culture of peace, environmentally sound sustainable development, social cohesion, and international citizenship. Successful vocational education schemes are usually designed with inherent and built-in links with higher educational and occupational levels, through the formal or non-formal systems of education, within the general concept of continuing and lifelong education. In some education systems, especially those of developing countries, the realisation of this concept would necessitate the restructuring and reform of higher education, in order to eliminate bottlenecks, and establish lateral and vertical channels among the various fields and levels of educational and training offerings, to promote occupational and educational mobility and, consequently social mobility.

The dynamics and changing demand of the labour market require more and more the replacement of physical skills by mental skills, and hence the vocation education schemes and programmes be liberalised and broad-based, to promote adaptability, widen the scope of job opportunities, and enhance educational and occupational mobility. Vocational education, should do more than provide the learner with the specific skills and knowledge needed for the job. It should be acknowledged that occupations are more effectively performed by workers who are generally, as well as specifically prepared, taking into consideration the ongoing transformation of work processes, technologies and environments. The social status of vocational education can be enhanced in practice through appropriate career guidance and counselling services, as well as employment and placement services.

The book reviews the current status of vocational guidance programmes available and presents the trends and future orientations in this field. It provides examples for the goals and essential elements of a policy on guidance; descriptions of major components of a guidance programme including curriculum-based career guidance, individual career planning, counselling service replying to students' needs, etc. It outlines the responsibilities for guidance on the part of educational administrators, counsellors, and teachers.

Editor

Contents

Preface — *v*

1. **Introduction** — 1
Role of Urbanisation • Information Technology • Open and Distance Learning • Educational Technology • Early school leavers • Girls and women • ODL Technologies and Media.

2. **Academic Standards in Vocational Education** — 13
Alternative Education.

3. **Potential Learners and Articulation** — 26
TVET Programme in ODL • Rationalising the Delivery of TVET Through ODL • Mobility and Articulation • Importance of Articulation and its Impact on Mobility • National Priorities • Barriers to Articulation • India: Unresolved Constraints to Articulation • Articulation Arrangements • National Need and Individual Aspirations • Change of Postsecondary Education • Information Technology Educational Implications • The Role of Private Education • The International Dimension of

Articulation • Australia • Technical and Vocational Education • Articulation • Indonesia • Postsecondary Technical and Vocational Education • Malaysia • Postsecondary Technical and Vocational Education • Industrial Training Institutes • National Youth Training Institutes • Polytechnics • MARA Institute of Technology (ITM) • Universities • Private TVE institutions • The Philippines • Postsecondary Technical and Vocational Education • The Objectives of TESDA are to Articulation • Singapore • Technical and Vocational Education • Polytechnics • Institute of Technical Education • LaSalle SIA College of the Arts • SHATEC • Singapore Institute of Management • Private Business and Computer Colleges • Thailand • Postsecondary Technical and Vocational Education • Non-formal Vocational Education.

4. **Vocational Education and Training in 21st Century** 98

New Technologies and the Production Process • Implications for Technical and Vocational Education and Training • Continuing Training • New Technologies and the Production Process • New Technologies—Vocational Education and Training.

5. **Guidance Counsellor** 124

Educational Guidance and Counselling • Career and Vocational Guidance and Counselling • Individualized Career-path Planning • Employment Placement •

Personal Guidance and Counselling • Individual Counselling • Group Counselling • Developmental Programmes • Information Gathering and Dissemination • Information and Communications Technology (ICT) • Re-structured Senior Cycle and the Guidance Counsellor • A New Senior Cycle • Guidance Context • Origins of restructuring • Perceptions of the Counsellor's Role • Historical Legacies • Principal's Perceptions • Counsellor as Collaborator • The Guidance Perspective • Transition Year Guidelines • Leaving Certificate Vocational Programme (LCVP) • Challenges for the Counsellor.

6. **Open and Distance** 150
Tutoring • Technology and Student Support • Audio-based Technologies • Video-based Technologies • Computer-based Technologies • Virtual Campuses • The Curriculum • Philosophical Approaches • Constructivism • Essential Skills • Learning Resources.

7. **Strategies in Vocational Education** 173
Planning for an ODL Programme • Keep it Simple • Select a Team • Teaching Practical Skills • Learning Practical Skills • Learning Materials • Video • CD-ROM • Online • Learning Environments • Assessment • Formative Assessment • Summative Assessment • Gathering Evidence • Workplace Trainers and Assessors • Delivering the Programme • Adoption Technology • Flexible Learning - anywhere, any Place, any Time.

8. Methods of Vocational Education 203
Process Learning • Social Learning • Learning to Plan • Didactic Models • On-the-job Training • • Course Instruction • Learning in School-run Enterprises • The Concept of Modules of Employable Skills (MES) Training.

Appendix
Revised Recommendation Concerning Technical and Vocational Education 233

Bibliography 278

Index 280

1

Introduction

Today, things are not so simple. The present requirements are characterised by high technology on the one hand, and basic human survival on the other, depending on where live. Accordingly, the needs for skills and knowledge as well as the modality of education and training may vary. Yet society is moving in a direction that demands high levels of knowledge and skill in information and communication technology, biotechnology, global business and commercial practices, transport and conveyance, maintenance of law and order and various other aspects of day-to-day living. Degrading environment, dwindling energy reserves, shortage of clean water and basic health needs are some of the other problems with tremendous implications on skills development. Further, rapidly growing populations in many countries has increased not only the demand for resources but has caused other problems affecting quality of life such as finding germ-free water and food, adequate energy and power, clothing and shelter. Setting priorities is not easy for many countries, but developing nations face a greater challenge. To them it is not a question of addressing one challenge over the other, but of tackling all problems at the same time. In other words, economic development is not only related to employment and training but also to development as a whole, inclusive of economic and social dimensions.

Therefore, technical and vocational education and training (TVET) should include both social and productive skills. The list of different skills and knowledge areas needed is endless, but the point that highly skilled personnel are needed in the foundations of a developed society today cannot be missed. In complex society the process of development involves all people, and all must be skilled and educated for this process.

Role of Urbanisation

Urbanisation is largely a phenomenon of the 20th century. Large urban conglomerations have developed all over the world and their future exponential expansion threatens the quality of life on earth. The urban lifestyle is a matter of grave concern in terms of supplies, sewage and garbage disposal, energetics, transport and environmental quality. Cities have not only been drawing the human population by migration from rural areas, but have also been sucking the precious life-supporting resources of the earth disproportionately to the land area they occupy. TVET has contributed to the development of urban civilisation and must now reorient itself to make our cities better habitat. Providing a comfortable life of better quality in rural areas is one possible solution, but it demands developing appropriate skills in all people. Urbanisation and humanity's desire to exploit nature for its needs and comforts is also the cause of high consumption of resources.

Once a new developmental paradigm is defined, it would become imperative to review our priorities and to make skills development comprehensive as well as visible, through a pervasiveness in our education and training systems.

Sustainable development essentially means establishing a pattern of development which conserves the natural resources of the earth for unlimited use by future generations, preventing environmental degradation and, to the extent possible, finding alternative sources of energy and materials. Human activities today are consuming precious natural resources and degrading the environment on a scale never seen before. The very life support system on earth has been endangered. Rapidly increasing populations in many of the developing countries, and the western pattern of development they are emulating, have much to do with this devastating trend. There are manifold manifestations of this problem, such as global climatic imbalances, depletion of biodiversity and forest cover, food and water shortages, and health-related problems to name a few. It is not enough to understand the problem and apply long-term correctives. There are immediate implications on skills development, particularly in rural areas of developing countries.

Training is needed now to address the issues of renewable energy generation, management of water both for healthful living and farming, sustainable agriculture, etc. For both economic and social development, immediate skills development is needed on a very large scale. What is required of the delivery method for such education and training is a vastly expanded system consisting of both formal and open learning, which would have to resort to distance learning modalities.

Information Technology

Information technology (IT) which marks the post-agrarian and industrial phase of civilisation. Even in existing agrarian economies of today, IT is being used increasingly, and there is an overwhelming desire to 'jump on the IT bandwagon' to compete with the developed world. This change-over marks the increasing use of information in the production of goods and services as well as in day-to-day living. Information and the ability to process and use it are the keys to global power balance, economic or political. The extending frontiers, expanding capabilities and innovations in the application of information, lead us to an unforeseeable future—friendly or frightening but something to co-exist with. The implications for TVET in this scenario are enormous.

The growth of IT and related developments in the recent past have turned the world into a global marketplace. Gradually, national and regional economies are transforming into a single global economy. This economic interdependence means that in the future will swim or sink together. Globalisation has given birth to intense international competition to expand trade and commerce and a desire on the part of every country to capture as much of the global consumer market as possible. All this demands superior skills of production, distribution and communication as never seen before in the history of the human race. New skills are being demanded today, necessitated by competitive participation in the new economic world order.

Open and Distance Learning

There has been a concurrent development in the field of education. The contact mode of instruction in the closed education system is no more the sole modality of learning. Open and distance learning (ODL) is well in place throughout the world and is fast gaining social acceptability. Within the overall educational framework, the acquisition of marketable skills and competence for employability have come to assume a critical role in the technologically changing world. It is no longer enough to have traditionally literate (or illiterate) people earning their living from subsistence farming. What is needed is a large base of skilled people capable not only of performing at a given time, but also of continually upgrading their capabilities to meet the changing demands of future.

In many developing countries the process of development in the last half century has left a majority of illiterate, unskilled and uneducated people outside its fold. Any future development in these countries must aim to build a solid foundation of a technically skilled workforce. If the developing countries want to enhance their international competitiveness for the well-being of their people, they must address the concern for TVET. The path to economic development and prosperity is through skills training, and ODL as the modality for TVET allows vast numbers of people, hitherto unreached, to take advantage of education and training opportunities.

Distance education is defined as 'teaching and learning in which learning normally occurs at a different place from teaching.' Further, distance education courses are 'structured programmes of instruction for a learner in a different place from a teacher, having learning objectives, one or more teachers, a medium of communication and subject matter.' The distance education system has all the component processes that result in distance education, including learning, teaching, communication design and management. But that definition leaves out open learning. With its roots in correspondence education, ODL is an evolving concept of recent origin. Its various ramifications and its true meaning should not be searched for in a dictionary. 'Open' has to be understood against the backdrop of 'closed' or 'formal,' and 'distance' against the ideas of 'contact' or 'face to face.' Essentially, ODL does not mean group learning that takes place under the supervision of a teacher in a formal classroom situation. In distance learning the learner and teacher are spatially and temporally separated, and the use of electronic media or educational technology is prevalent.

ODL provides learner autonomy, which means flexibility in the time and place of learning, as well as in the speed or pacing of learning. Learners may be given a free option of courses within a given specialisation and also embrace choice in terms of technology. Learners may use print or electronic media that may include one or more of computer, TV, video, radio, telephone, e-mail and fax.

Educational Technology

Educational technology, so commonly used in both conventional learning and ODL, is of greater interest. If the teacher is physically absent, a substitute must be found for the powerful mode of personal communication —the human words, gesture, eye contact or body language. The choice of media provides an alternative, for better or worse. Many regard today's state-of-the-art technology as very efficient, while others hold that there can be no better substitute for the teacher.

ODL may be available through an organisation exclusively created for the purpose, such as an open university or open school, or through a conventional organisation offering both ODL and formal courses. Within each type of organisation, ODL may be offered in a variety of patterns. There are many ways in which ODL can impact TVET. While on the one hand it can enhance the participation of young and fresh learners, on the other it opens a totally new frontier for workers aspiring to improve their vertical mobility both academically and professionally. The learning groups that have been brought under sharper focus through ODL are diverse, and without ODL they would have been otherwise disadvantaged.

Early school leavers

There is an overwhelming number of children who, for a variety of reasons, never enter the school system or who drop out during the elementary cycle of education. To them the school curriculum is too theoretical or does not prepare them for life. These children generally enter the world of work ill-equipped and can earn only meagre wages. But if instead, along with theoretical instruction, practical marketable skills were taught to them, they might continue their studies in the hope of a better life.

Small or large clusters of habitations which formal schools often do not reach pose a challenge to the educational process. The facilities are poor, teachers absent and the skills of the modern world scarce. ODL techniques would be the most suited for learners in such places where TVET can reach most of these children who are socially and economically deprived. ODL would also benefit those children who find the school timing inconvenient and who would like to exercise some freedom and autonomy. With ODL they can study at their own pace and complete a programme stretching the usual time boundary.

Girls and women

Girls and women are generally characterised by poor participation in TVET, and changing that often proves to be a challenge. Girls and women make up nearly half the population, and a majority of them stay home where there is enormous scope for their profound social roles and economic productivity. Such a vast human resource can more efficiently be tapped through ODL, with the result, in some countries, of girls and women being the prime movers of development by virtue of their improved insight into social and economic aspects. ODL-TVET has the greatest potential in this respect.

ODL is of much advantage to employed workers who wish to enhance their educational or professional equipment, but who are not in a position to attend school full-time within the given rigid framework. It suits such students because they can enrol part-time and complete the requirements in a more flexible situation. They can also work on part of a given programme on a course-to-course basis for which they may not attend classes. They can learn while working without any loss of time. Almost all countries have laid down policy postulates concerning ODL articulated in one form or another. There are certain common features in all of them which relate to one or more of these issues:

— Financing
— Regional and socio-economic disparities
— Provision by private or public providers
— Separate institutional framework versus integrated educational system
— Certification and accreditation
— Promoting and providing technologies for ODL
— Co-ordination between media and educational sectors.

The following descriptions provide a general presentation of some of these policy parameters which may have bearing on ODL.

Financing: The political commitment to and national policy on ODL must be reflected through liberal financing. The basic question in financing relates to the competition between traditional learning and ODL on the one hand, and general education versus TVET on the other. ODL is still a new idea in the educational arena and many national governments would like to be convinced of the pay-off that might accrue in the long- and short-term. The traditional school and university systems are much too well anchored with often strong lobbies that would resist any reduction in their share of available resources. The same thing is true for general education as opposed to TVET. These aspects impact the support behind TVET through ODL, particularly in developing countries. However, in view of the growing international significance of both ODL and TVET, and because internationalisation of ODL is an inevitable trend and almost all developing countries would like to achieve national development at a rapid pace, the scale tends to tilt towards ODL. The international donor agencies and promoters of educational development continue to enhance significantly the national policy support to ODL.

In most developing countries ODL is seen as being of special benefit to the 'left out' and deprived learners. As these groups are unable to meet the high cost of private institutions, the national governments take upon themselves the role of TVET provider. Yet the demand in certain trades is so overwhelming that private providers readily jump into the fray with the desire to 'make hay while the sun shines.' These providers are often regulated by the state and sometimes by international institutions, which gives their graduates an opening into the international job market.

Very often the private TVET institutions delivering their programmes have their own system of student certification. At the same time the countries put in place their own public system of recognition and accreditation. However, the public system is characterised by some mode of centralised evaluation and certification. Their degrees are automatically accredited for jobs in both private and public sectors. From the point of view of quality, the private providers generally perform better and have a higher rating. The policy question, therefore, is how to maintain the comparability of quality and how to have a system of certification and accreditation that is internationally acceptable.

ODL Technologies and Media

ODL cannot be provided without resorting to advanced and appropriate technologies. Co-ordination has to be established between more traditional media sectors like TV and radio on the one hand, and newer information and communication technologies (ICTs), such as e-mail, telephone and fax, on the other. Because ODL is inter-sectoral in nature, national policy support is inevitable and impacts teaching/learning through the ODL system.

TVET through ODL requires more than instructors at a distance. For certain components of the programme, learner support has to be through physical contact, either in classrooms at a distance or on workplace sites of production of goods or services. This requirement, also being inter-sectoral, has to be achieved through policy directives laid down either nationally or locally.

Over the past 25 years or so, ODL has been driven mostly by learners' needs and the diversification of media used in instruction. Many of the educational technologies, such as e-mail, fax, video and audio-video conferencing, have arrived on the scene during this period. The same period has also witnessed the phenomenon of mass participation of diverse groups in the educational process. The diversifying clientele has brought the educational planners to defining and formulating a variety of curricula to meet its needs. The accent on TVET delivered through ODL, as opposed to the conventional programmes in the formal education system, has emerged as a direct consequence. A new paradigm of sustainable development where the natural resources are judiciously consumed; energy, water and productivity of the land conserved; and the overall ecology respected is seen to change the content of TVET in both developed and developing countries in the future. The other notable changes in the field of information technology as well as globalisation of economy have had a great impact on TVET. The international and national policy support for TVET through ODL has been forthcoming in ample measure, and the future expansion as well as qualitative changes in this area are going to be further demand-driven.

2

Academic Standards in Vocational Education

The high academic standards movement is based on the proposition that all students should be held to high academic standards and should have opportunities to achieve at these higher levels. This core principle is based on the understanding that, to succeed in the new economy, all students need better reasoning, problem-solving, and communication skills-knowledge and skills that students should gain in the K-12 education system. Since the standards movement began in the late 1980s, all states but one have adopted statewide standards in at least two core academic subjects, and most are implementing assessments to measure student attainment of the standards. Some of those assessments are high-stakes-students must pass the tests to graduate or to be promoted to the next grade. About half the states are implementing high-stakes tests for high school graduation. Only a few are using them for promotion decisions. States are also creating systems for holding students, teachers, and schools accountable for student learning. Despite the benefits believed to result from holding all students to high standards, policymakers and educators are discovering that the successful implementation of high academic standards presents challenges.

Successful implementation of high academic standards requires new curricular and instructional materials aligned to state standards; quality instruction; improved teacher training programs; and strategic, high-quality professional development. States have made significant strides, but many of these reforms have not yet reached the classroom in meaningful ways. Teachers have varying levels of knowledge about state standards. Many have received little training or assistance in developing instructional practices to help students meet standards while, at the same time, they feel the pressures of accountability systems that hold them responsible for student learning. Nevertheless, in states where standards, classroom instruction, and tests are aligned, students are rising to the occasion and meeting the rigors of high standards. State policymakers and education officials are also discovering that certain populations of students present unique challenges.

The Individuals with Disabilities Education Act (IDEA) requires states to include all students in the state assessment program-including students with special needs and those in alternative programs, who have traditionally been excluded from state assessments. For students with disabilities or limited English proficiency, the law does allow special accommodations, such as special time allowances, larger-print tests, and multilingual tests. Many students in alternative education programmes have learning disabilities or special needs and may be eligible for similar accommodations. However, the requirement that most, if not all, students be included in state testing is new and will require alternative programs to prepare students to take and pass the tests. To help students succeed, alternative programs may need to make significant changes in curricula and instruction. The impact that high academic standards and aligned assessments and instruction will have on traditional and nontraditional educational systems and on student learning and achievement remains largely unknown because standards, assessments, and accountability systems are still being implemented in many states.

Some critics argue that high-stakes tests, in particular, will have an adverse impact on the depth of student learning by pressuring teachers to narrow the curriculum and 'teach to the test'-emphasizing rote memorization of expected test items and test-taking strategies—at the expense of deeper curricula and higher-order thinking skills. Educators in alternative settings also have concerns that in a high-stakes system, students already at—risk of school failure will be more prone to drop out of traditional education programs, thereby increasing the overall demand for an already limited number of slots in alternative education programs. Both concerns point to the need for strong teacher preparation and professional development that are connected to state standards and offer multiple instructional strategies for helping students learn the content outlined in the standards.

State accountability systems can play an integral role in ensuring that all parts of the system work to create higher expectations for all students and provide the opportunities and resources students need to meet the standards. Whatever the challenges, advocates argue that, as a matter of equality and opportunity, all students should be held to high standards and given the chance to succeed.

Alternative Education

Alternative education programmes include all educational programmes that fall outside the traditional K-12 school system. However, focuses primarily on alternative education programs that serve school-aged students who have dropped out of high school. Alternative education programmes offer diplomas, General Educational Development (GED) diplomas, and certificates and are operated by a number of different organisations, including community-based organisations (CBOs), school districts, adult-education divisions. Alternative education programmes are a crucial element of states' public education systems. They provide an option to educate students for whom traditional education systems are responsible but may be ineffective. Typically, students enrolled in alternative education programmes are older and face a range of issues—e.g., involvement in the criminal- or juvenile-justice system, pregnancy, parenting, substance abuse, and learning disabilities—that may have contributed to their exit from traditional school systems. Many of these youth have also not been effectively taught early in their academic careers and are far behind their age-appropriate grade level.

Alternative education programmes fill an important role by providing 'second chance' opportunities for these students. Despite the importance of alternative education, there is a remarkable lack of comprehensive information about the number and quality of alternative educational programmes and the numbers, demographics, and type of students served. This lack of information presents a major challenge in a number of areas, including determining the adequacy of supply and demand for alternative education slots. Although there is no definitive count, estimates indicate that approximately 200,000 alternative education programme slots are available nationwide and that only about 5 percent of all out-of-school youth are enrolled in some type of alternative education program. Around 18,000 students were enrolled in 868 programmes and schools. Of these, 13,000 were enrolled in high school—8 percent of the state's total enrollment—and about 2,800 were enrolled in alternative middle schools. In addition to collecting this type of information, the state is also making efforts to assess the quality of its alternative education programs and recently passed a law.

Alternative educational programmes differ from traditional high schools in a number of ways, including following nontraditional school hours and schedules; having open admission and open exit policies; and tailoring instruction to the individual needs of the student. Perhaps the most distinguishing characteristic of quality alternative programmes, however, is their reliance on youth development principles to organize coursework and curricula. This includes the development of curricula that are focused on the development of essential competencies and skills, including so called 'soft skills.' This also includes a focus on the development of job skills and work experience. This strong connection to the world of work is a vital component of the curriculum of many alternative education programs.

The General Educational Development (GED) Test. Any discussion of the impact of high standards on alternative education programmes must also include mention of the GED. The GED, the credential attained by many students in alternative educational programs, is in the process of being revised to reflect new state standards; a new version is due to be released in 2002. The 2002 GED test will cover core academic areas similar to those in earlier versions but will also include more 'business-related and adult-context information.' Students taking the new GED will be affected by high standards in two ways: the new tests themselves will mirror the high standards for secondary education, and minimum passing scores will be normed to high school seniors who have been educated within a high-standards system. The awarding of GED diplomas is increasing at the same time that the national high school graduation rate is declining. Currently, one in seven high school 'graduates' in this country actually holds a GED. Last year alone, 500,000 GEDs were awarded, and the GED Testing Service—the group responsible for the design and administration of the test-predicts that by 2002, 1 million individuals will take the GED annually.

Although the GED was originally developed as a means to help veterans advance to postsecondary educational opportunities, the majority of individuals who receive a GED today do not progress to postsecondary education. Alternative Education and High Academic Standards: Opportunities and Concerns Despite the large and growing number of students in alternative education programs, particularly in urban areas, alternative education programs have generally fallen outside the high academic standards movement. However, many states are beginning to require ali students to pass state tests to receive a diploma, causing policymakers to examine strategically the impact that high standards will have on alternative education. If the high academic standards movement is to improve learning and academic outcomes for all students, high standards need to be implemented in alternative programs. And although students in alternative education programs can significantly raise their academic achievement, they can do so only in quality programmes that provide tailored instruction that meets their individual needs. Without this flexibility and customized approach, the effectiveness of these programs will be greatly reduced. Policymakers should be aware of a number of issues relating to alternative education as they move forward with implementing standards-based education reform.

— *Testing issues:* Because many alternative education students have special needs—e.g., learning disabilities and language deficiencies-alternative education programmes will be disproportionately affected by the need to provide special testing accommodations. Additionally, because many alternative education students are older and may be difficult to place in a specific grade, age- and grade-specific standardized tests for graduation and accountability may need to be more flexible. It will fall to alternative programs to identify these students and provide ways to test them that are both fair and consistent with high standards. Although appropriate assessment is not unique to alternative education programs, given the population of youth that these programs serve and the disproportionate numbers of students with special needs, this will be a tremendous task.

— *Higher dropout rates of alternative Sstudents:* Alternative education programmes are tailored to the specific needs of individual students—this is their hallmark. Alternative educators are concerned that rigid introduction of high academic standards and high-stakes tests may affect an alternative programme's ability to provide flexible and tailored instruction, thereby causing these students to fail academically, become frustrated, and drop out of school. In such instances, it is important to recognize and document student academic achievements and learning, and to help these students build on gains over time.

— *School accountability:* In a high academic standards environment, schools are held accountable for the attainment of their students and funding may be contingent on outcomes. However, programme completion rates and student academic achievement, in terms of numbers and percentage of diplomas awarded, may not be accurate or fair assessments of a programme's performance. The reasons students drop out of traditional schools are myriad and include such things as pregnancy, health issues, need for employment, incarceration, substance abuse, and learning disabilities. For students who are unable to succeed in traditional educational settings, alternative education programs provide an invaluable and singular service. However, many of these individuals will also have difficulties succeeding in alternative programs. It may take them several attempts to complete their diploma or GED. It may take them much longer to finish than in a traditional program, and some may enroll in several different programs before attaining success. Accountability systems for all schools are stronger and fairer when they are based on multiple measures of student achievement and improvement. Clear and rigorous standards and aligned, reliable, valid assessments form the bases for such an accountability system.

— *Teacher training and professional development:* Although concerns about academic standards and teacher quality are by no means unique to alternative education, high academic standards present some very particular challenges to alternative education programmes. All teachers need additional professional development opportunities to improve instruction and incorporate state standards, but those in alternative programs may need more. Alternative education teachers often are not certified, may lack instructional training, and may have had few opportunities to learn about the new standards and how to implement them effectively for students with diverse needs. Additionally, because alternative education programs are often structured very differently than traditional schools, training and development activities around the new standards will have to be customized for alternative education programmes.

To ensure a smooth transition to high standards, alternative education programs also will need additional resources to develop curricula and materials and to train teachers. Although this issue is not unique to alternative education programs, alternative programs are at an enormous disadvantage because they often lack networks and other external support structures found in large-scale, traditional school systems. States need to consider ways to improve funding for existing alternative education programs and to fund additional ones, especially as only 5 percent of dropouts are served. One possible funding strategy for a state to consider is the expansion of the role of charter schools. Another is to permit state resources to follow students from traditional to nontraditional settings.

Policymakers implementing high academic standards should recognize the real value of alternative education programs in meeting the needs of nontraditional students. Although alternative education students may need some accommodations, they should be given the same opportunity to demonstrate that they can meet the high standards that traditional students must meet. There are a number of actions states can take to improve students' likelihood of success.

— Strengthen links between traditional and nontraditional education systems. States need to recognize that alternative education programs are essential to fulfilling their mission to provide fair and equal educational opportunities to all students. Most alternative education programs are unfortunately at a distinct disadvantage in terms of providing the necessary up-front and ongoing resources to improve instruction and curricular materials and in providing instructors with training opportunities to help them adapt to a high-standards environment. Traditional schools should share best practices and lessons learned from their experience in implementing standards-based curricula with their alternative education counterparts. States should include alternative educators in their statewide training efforts and should also provide customized professional training opportunities designed to meet their specific needs. By supporting the two-way sharing of best practices between traditional and nontraditional education systems, including ways that personalized educational approaches developed by alternative education programs can be adopted in traditional education settings, states can help reduce dropout rates and improve student performance in both traditional and alternative settings.

— Invest resources to support the transition to high academic standards and beyond. Implementing high standards in alternative education programs will require additional up-front and ongoing resources to improve instruction and curricular materials, and to provide instructors with necessary training.

— Improve 'early warning systems' to identify lower-performing students. States that have already implemented standards-based reforms have learned that students at risk of failure and dropping out need extra attention and support to succeed. This support is most effective when delivered early in a student's academic career, before the student falls behind the age-appropriate grade level. In introducing high academic standards, states should aim to improve their early warning systems-using standards, aligned assessments, data and feedback from tests, and new instructional strategies-to better identify and support these struggling students.

— Support longer-term alternative education programs. Many alternative education programs are designed to be short-term in nature. Raising the academic achievement of youth who are already well behind grade level-e.g., a ninth-grade youth with a fourth-grade reading level-in a relatively short time may not be realistic. Meeting the rigors of high academic standards in this short time present an additional challenge. States should consider ways to extend the length of alternative education programs to provide youth with the opportunity to significantly raise their academic achievement within a high academic environment.

— Develop data-driven accountability measures for alternative education programs. Holding alternative schools accountable only for their passing rates on high-stakes tests or their program completion rates does not take into account the full measure of their worth. There is value in collecting this information, however. Accountability systems based on multiple measures that reflect individual student achievement and improvement, that consider the open admission and exit policies of many alternative education programmes, and that consider the delivery of ancillary services, such as counselling, substance—abuse services, job training, and employment rates, may provide better indications of programme performance. Student performance on the statewide tests is one measure of student achievement. Strong accountability systems rely on additional measures of student achievement and learning, such as teacher-designed, classroom-based assessments, student attendance, and possibly job performance or demonstrations of job-related learning.

Data on alternative education programs and students are, for the most part, incomplete and fragmented. Policymakers are making decisions on very limited information and without good indicators of current trends. To make more informed decisions and to promote accountability, states need to collect data on alternative education programs, the students they serve, their performance on statewide assessments and other achievement indicators, and on the teachers who work in these settings.

3

Potential Learners and Articulation

The meaning of 'potential learners,' it is unhelpful to dissociate them from their environment, more so because the economic well-being of the respective countries in which they live vary. Also, existing national educational provision and economic and social services are essential contributory factors worthy of consideration. More relevant, perhaps, is that the dictates of the national job market should serve as an indicator for the skills needed for sustenance and potential national economic development. Ignoring all these attendant influences in national development where diverse economic backgrounds dictate their respective national policies would only result in an incomplete picture of the status quo.

The study of potential learners using the open and distance learning (ODL) mode for technical and vocational education and training (TVET) programme/ qualifications cannot be considered in isolation from the countries from which the ODL institutions operate or, indeed, from the kinds of programmes they offer. The increasing interest in globalisation of education might change the direction of national policies, especially within the economically disadvantaged countries, but there is evidence to suggest that ODL practitioners in some of these countries are as attuned to concerns of access and quality as are practitioners in the North.

Issues of quality, access and variety are much in evidence among concerns of ODL institutions and practitioners in Asia, where enforcement of standards of quality is embedded in the national policies of some countries and where economies of scale are much more successfully realised than in sub-Saharan Africa and the many small states in the Commonwealth. Much of the analysis here of the issues regarding potential learners using ODL for TVET programmes concentrates, therefore, on developments within the Commonwealth. This group of nations reflects a microcosm of the rest of the world in terms of cultural and socio-economic mix, and so conclusions reached will have relevance beyond geographical boundaries. Given also that the majority of the countries in the Commonwealth are economically disadvantaged, the laissez-faire approach that dominates choice exercised by potential learners in economically advantaged countries does not exist in the rest of the Commonwealth or in those countries with a similar economic background. Here, choice is not only restricted to those who can afford to pay.

Some of the TVET programmes offered are directed and driven more by design for the benefit of targeted groups or communities than for individuals. Planned training provided in this way makes specific impact on the economic welfare of those targeted audiences, whether community groups or special workers. As planned development programmes, they often have their basis in health or agriculture and their impact offer some measure of sustainability where none existed previously. Within the context of TVET programmes for potential learners, however, a much wider range of skills training is not only expected but is also inevitable. This will not preclude more of them continuing to be planned programmes as some of them have been in the past.

TVET Programme in ODL

Considering the impact of TVET cadre of staff anywhere as the lifeblood of service of the region, their value to their respective regions' economic well-being must be regarded as no less than its mainstay for wealth creation and accumulation. Within this context, potential learners who would benefit from TVET programmes offered through ODL cut across a wide range of educational, social and economic levels. One of the largest target groups, particularly within the developing world, is that of illiterate people. With 72% of all the illiterate people in the world living in nine high-population countries, any planned ODL programmes for potential learners realising a measure of success in those specific countries alone would have a substantial impact on their economies. Also worth mentioning is that teenagers will comprise the single largest group in the world in the next 20 years.

In the developing South, this has already been realised and the level of unemployment among the young is very high. Implementing TVET programmes through ODL will not only transform the economic power of the beneficiaries, the weak economies of the South will improve considerably. Indeed, TVET programmes offer better opportunities for skills training where beneficiaries could become self-employed or established in family enterprises. Given the claim that half of the world's employed labour force is in that category, the long-term implication is that training offered in a variety of locally targeted but employable job possibilities could equip a large proportion of illiterate and unskilled people with employable skills. There is ample evidence supporting the potential of ODL delivery systems as being appropriate for equipping illiterates with skills.

TVET programmes offered through ODL need not apply to just those examples mentioned. TVET also responds readily to the introduction of the Internet for more sophisticated ODL approaches to learning, which reflects the other end of the spectrum where course designers develop and modify teaching strategies for a better student-centred approach with greater beneficial consequences.

Rationalising the Delivery of TVET Through ODL

The effectiveness of the ODL delivery mechanisms has been very well rehearsed. The so-called three generations of ODL practice are still in use, each considered appropriate and effective in their respective contexts. The question, therefore, of utilising an appropriate ODL delivery method for potential learners offering TVET programmes depends largely on other factors, such as the institution hosting the delivery of the programme, resources available and infrastructure requirements. Given the socio-economic structures of countries in the Commonwealth, even those in the South may require differing delivery methods for TVET programmes. Where national or regional arrangements are adopted, articulating the issues beyond the confines of the institution responsible would bring out the merits or otherwise of one method as against another.

The idea of establishing multi-channel distance learning centres within Africa for use by ODL practitioners in the continent was mooted in 1995—an ideal concept that might have resulted in the development of TVET programmes for all sub-Saharan Africa. In spite of its relevance for this purpose, the pace and widespread use of ICT in ODL practice provides another dimension to the delivery of TVET programmes for potential learners. There are many advantages to the idea of a network situation where programmes could be accessed by potential learners in several countries. The increasing spread of globalisation of ODL offers the idea of lifelong learning a lifeline across national boundaries, despite economically disadvantaged countries feeling threatened. Furthermore, the potential of launching TVET programmes to a mass audience must have appeal to the volume of beneficiaries. Its merit lies in the immediacy of its impact and the prospect it offers of quality programmes for potential learners whose economic transformation would be widespread with lasting repercussions beyond the individuals themselves.

Speaking from an idealistic standpoint, everyone is a potential learner. The move towards the idea of lifelong learning has developed a force of its own that suggests inclusion rather than exclusion. ODL institutions in the prosperous North are expanding their horizons with increasing use of information and communication technology (ICT) as a means of delivery. Potential learners in the North have a lead in the use of the technology that could result in 'technology leapfrogging' for potential learners in the South. Globalisation as a general concept in world trade, finance and now in education is a fluid phenomenon whose impact on the world stage has been described as operating in a Darwinian framework. So, in terms of its appropriateness for the disadvantaged economies of the South, one can speculate about both its worthiness for TVET programmes and how long it will be before it is implemented.

There are a number of factors to consider when attempting to assess the viability of globilisation as a mode of delivery for potential learners of TVET programmes. For example, its impact on the economy of countries in the South has, historically, been negative. This has lead to the vulnerable economies of the developing Commonwealth countries being suspicious from the onset. In fact, the impact on ODL practices arising from World Bank/IMF structural adjustment policies, particularly in the case of recipients of loans in African countries, has adversely affected quality. The evidence of globalisation continues to offer threat to the pessimists, thus making its appropriateness for the delivery of TVET programmes to potential learners a questionable prospect in the immediate future for some countries. However, another view of globalisation is that it offers positive challenges for the general development of weaker national economies. Potential learners in such environments are seen to have a lot to gain from TVET programmes using the ODL mode.

Consequently, the best solution for those countries is to look for creative economic ideas which combine their well-being, in terms of income-generating schemes, and the political will for good governance. For example, implementation of regional intra-trade policies has been identified as a positive force in minimising the impact of global influence on the national economy. In that context, the view that some countries in the South are 'almost integrated into the globalised economy' may serve as a pointer for what is achievable for all countries in the South. Infrastructure deficiency is usually offered as the main cause of the problem with ODL provision in all sub-regions in the South, even though the factors affecting their respective sub-regional infrastructure may be different. Thus it is possible that differences in economic performance in a South-South context may not always militate against the globalisation of TVET programmes by ODL. Evidence can be adduced in support of this view, particularly in Asia, where seven of the 12 'dynamic developing countries' in the world are located. There, per capita incomes today are at least seven times what they were in 1960. Given also that the concept of globalisation is regarded as market driven, its strength for countries in the developing South may be found in joint ventures and co-operative schemes, whether political, educational or commercial, that provide the force to minimise the Darwinian effect mentioned earlier.

Global ODL delivery of TVET programmes to potential learners has a much stronger prospect of being realised sooner in the Asia sub-region than some may expect. Further support has been adduced by evidence of buoyant trade results in Asia and Latin America where, economic and political ties have strengthened over a period of time. In turn, co-operation in matters of politics, commerce and education, including ODL, has encouraged the growth of regionalisation against the impact of globalisation. The effect has created a level of commitment which has fostered political stability and nurtured standardisation of good management practice. Such a record of regional co-operation, political stability and vigorous intra-trade practice offers a good prospect of effecting global TVET programmes by ODL to potential learners in those regions.

Looking at the scenario posed by the sub-regions of the South, it is true that some regions are better prepared than others for ODL globalisation of TVET programmes to their potential learners. However, there must be no blanket disregard for its implementation on a sub-regional basis, considering its potential to empower marginalised groups. Development theorists tend to favour implementing programmes and policies which push human and economic activities beyond predictable levels of achievement and immediate comprehension. The possibilities of human endeavour thrive better under conditions offering challenges than in those situations where pace is either stagnant or slow. In the former context, technology 'leapfrogging' offers scope to those economic environments where the challenges of globalisation are daunting and where human aspirations are not restricted by rigid parameters. In the latter context, recipients of skills acquired may have achieved limited economic empowerment, but do not appear to be able to alleviate their communities/societies from poverty.

The Asian sub-region, on the basis of factors discussed earlier, is the hallmark of economic progress and vibrancy that conforms to the challenges of globalisation. It is, therefore, not outrageous to presume that global ODL provision of TVET programmes to potential learners is within the political and economic bounds of the Asian sub-region. At the same time, there are countries in the South that could offer similar TVET programmes by ODL using less sophisticated delivery mechanisms by being equally effective for their local conditions. ODL offers enough flexibility that potential learners anywhere can benefit from TVET programmes, whether on a large scale or not. The pre-conditions for technology 'leapfrogging' seem to have a basis in economic development and regional co-operation. The African sub-region requires political stability to encourage such requirements to take hold. With that, global ODL provision of TVET programmes to potential learners would have a better prospect of becoming a reality. In any case, other ODL delivery mechanisms have proven to be as equally effective, having withstood the test of time over several generations.

Mobility and Articulation

Articulation, in an educational sense, is the creation of pathways or linkages to facilitate the movement of students between programmes and institutions. The notion of a vocational education pathway implies passage through a series of educational experiences or employment-related competency formation, which aim to progress through to an occupational destination. Further pathways may then lead a way to another occupation. Educational articulation comes in different forms. For example, 'vertical' articulation could be the advancement of students from general education to technical and vocational education and training (TVET) programmes at polytechnics, technical institutes, community colleges, industry training centres, etc.

Another important form of articulation is the traffic of TVET graduates to programmes at universities or comparable institutions. Articulation can also exist within TVET systems or institutions. For example, students who successfully complete a skilled worker training programme might progress to a technician-level programme. Consider also the concept of 'reverse' articulation, which might take place when an individual who has partly or fully completed a university programme, or some other form of advanced studies, subsequently undertakes part or all of a TVET programme at a polytechnic or technical college. Reverse articulation may be the outcome of a university graduate deciding that he or she lacks practical knowledge or specific skills which are required for employment purposes, and which are conveniently available through a TVET institution. Such traffic is more likely when the status of TVET institutions as providers of relevant programmes in a community is high.

Successful articulation arrangements are often reflected in effective credit transfer practices. Credit transfer occurs when institutions agree to recognise the previous formal studies undertaken by a student and to grant to that student an agreed level of course credit for the new programme being enrolled in. Therefore, the receiving institution recognises that the student has previously achieved comparable knowledge and competencies to justify being given an exemption. Intertwined with the concept of articulation is 'recognition of the prior learning' (RPL) achieved by an individual. Such recognition is the sum of formal studies and other knowledge and competencies gained informally, perhaps as a result of skills acquired during employment. Well-structured systems of education will provide for acceptance of candidates for further study, who rely to some extent on RPL for entry to formal programmes of study, with or without some degree of advanced standing. Not all forms of articulation will result in credit transfer or RPL. There will be many instances where articulation simply results in the ability of a student to transfer from one programme to another without any credit being granted. Additionally, where a student does not satisfy entry requirements, some bridging studies may be necessary to redress any deficiencies.

Importance of Articulation and its Impact on Mobility

The development of education for the world of work in industrial societies during the 20th century has reflected to some extent Taylor's and Ford's notions of labour management and production methods based on rigid organisational control, with work being broken down into increasingly simplified tasks the further down the hierarchy an employee is located. Such notions have been compatible with the development and delivery of terminal courses of study in vocational education, on the basis that a person need only be trained to undertake a circumscribed range of tasks, with professionals and managerial staff directing and supervising work. Of course, Taylor's model of corporate organisation is still employed to some extent, particularly when production has been relocated to developing countries to take advantage of low wage costs. However, during recent decades, in the face of globalisation and the accompanying knowledge revolution, work has increasingly been re-engineered. Organisations tend to require adaptable and knowledgeable workers able to cope with change.

Staff need to be capable of working in teams and dealing with tasks and duties that overlap. Employers are seeking those who have a background that predisposes 'trainability' among their qualities. Therefore, the previously widely held notion that after an initial cycle of general education, followed by specialist studies or training for skilled work or a profession, the individual need not be overly concerned with further education or training, has proved to be incompatible with reality. Rapid and continuing change is now the norm in almost all fields of human endeavour. Jobs which have existed for long periods of time can simply disappear overnight. Changing occupational needs increasingly demand ongoing provision of lifelong learning, which may be a combination of formal courses, training or perhaps some form of on-the-job learning. The whole notion of lifelong learning encourages well-structured articulation arrangements and undermines the raison d'être for terminal courses of vocational education.

Effective articulation arrangements are a highly desirable feature of national educational offerings. Pathways created can directly influence the attractiveness of educational programmes and have considerable impact on participation rates and overall standings. In any case, an educational programme which is terminal in nature will be less attractive to potential students and their parents and be perceived as having a lower status than one which offers the possibility of realistic follow-on studies, either immediately or at a later time. Programmes which provide effective articulation arrangements will advance the educational and, subsequently, the occupational mobility of an individual. Relevant opportunities for articulation provide encouragement for the individual to capitalise on personal ability and enhance any possibility to conveniently move between occupations. These notions are not new. In 1964, the joint UNESCO/International Labour Organization Statement on Technical and Vocational Education and Training contended that TVET should be organised so that 'every person can continue his education until all his potentialities have been developed'.

National Priorities

National systems of education and training that offer effective articulation opportunities are in a better position to address issues of lifelong learning as the nature of work changes, rather than try to manage redundancy or unemployment. National policy-makers can play an important role by trying to ensure that, as much as possible, realistic educational pathways are embedded in overall systems of education and training at the planning stage, even if economic constraints or other strategic considerations limit full implementation until a later time. Many developing countries have ambitious objectives to establish new industries and service-oriented activities as quickly as possible. As a first step, low-cost, low-skill labour-intensive industries are frequently attractive. To move ahead to more rewarding economic outcomes, it is necessary for a country to increase the numbers of highly skilled personnel to support higher value-added industries. Such objectives are considerably more difficult to attain if the educational system does not have the capacity to upgrade its existing workforce to cope with new forms of work. Such is the nature of technological change: it is increasingly difficult to make long-term predictions on how to structure initial and recurrent forms of vocational education and training.

On one hand, industry often signals that individuals should be trained to undertake quite specific duties, and is frequently justifiably critical of the inability of TVET institutions or systems to translate industrial need into the competencies of programme graduates. Ideally, such objectives need to be harmonised with the needs of industry or commerce, but it is often difficult for educational authorities to predict labour market demands. Such criticism of TVET by industry and other stakeholders may be, in part, a reflection of defective linkages. Nevertheless, the dilemma for the TVET authorities is deciding how much they should structure educational programmes to address the perceived immediate needs of industry and commerce.

The main focus of TVET, regardless of whether it is provided through an upper secondary-level programme, technical college, community college, polytechnic or industry training centre, should be to assist an individual to gain occupational competencies in a specific field, with the aim of gaining employment as a skilled worker or technician/paraprofessional. This objective should not be at the expense of general education (except in the case of short-term training arrangements), because it is important that an individual has exposure to broader aspects of education. An objective should be to permit graduates of any programme to advance to further studies if they have the inclination and demonstrated ability to cope. On the other hand, if a programme of study is overly specialised, particularly if it is more or less focused on specific skills training, it is less likely to provide the sort of preparation that would assist in providing an individual with future options. Many countries have found that there is a significant mismatch between the output of TVET and higher education providers, and the needs of the labour market. This can result in severe unemployment or under-employment for programme graduates. It is important that seeking to provide articulated pathways to further study for TVET graduates is not done by expanding unemployment.

In many countries there is something of a fixation for the attainment of a university degree, with any other outcome being seen as a failure by both students and their parents. The provision of articulation pathway should not be seen as having as its main objective providing students with a mechanism to attain a degree, regardless of ability. Such an outcome should be one of a range of options available to students. It is not uncommon for students to enter a TVET programme after have been refused entry to a university. Such an outcome can trigger a feeling of failure in the individual. TVET programmes should be able to offer attractive pathways that can redress this situation and create an environment where the considerable expense incurred to that point, in both human and financial terms, can be redirected to the benefit of both the individual and the broader community. Developing nations, particularly those that are still largely agrarian, frequently find that the modern sector is incapable of absorbing the output of TVET or higher education institutions and providing wage-paying employment. When considering articulated pathway solutions in response to perceived need, preparation for other forms of work such as self-employment also need to be a high priority.

Barriers to Articulation

Countries that are at earlier stages of development may not perceive making effective articulation arrangements as an important objective. Indeed, in such instances the very opposite may be the case where demand for education at all levels is high and where places in all forms of post-secondary education are limited and subject to stringent competitive entry requirements.

In many developing countries, it is quite common for the available funds supporting education to be prioritised towards delivery of primary and secondary education, with limited provision for funding TVET and university-level education. But it is common in many developing countries for primary-level education to fall short of universal provision, and secondary-level education to be available only to limited numbers of students. Nevertheless, most countries aspire towards universal provision of primary and secondary education, and reasonably open access to TVET and higher education, because they realise the importance of working towards an effective system of education in the long term so they might fully participate in the global economy and lift overall national standards of living in a sustainable manner. Where barriers to articulation exist, they often appear at the interface between upper secondary vocational and university-level education.

This situation arises, in part, because the secondary vocational education may not have sufficient academic content, and consequently it is frequently not possible for graduates to proceed to regular university studies. Sometimes such difficulties may be mitigated by indirect pathways being made available, whereby the students may undertake a post-secondary technical education programme which ultimately offers some prospect of further studies. The same type of barrier frequently frustrates articulation arrangements between post-secondary TVET programmes and higher-level studies. Even though a graduate of a polytechnic or community college may have done well, the possibility of articulation to a related undergraduate degree may be very low or non-existent. This occurs because quota systems effectively preclude TVET graduates from transferring, with or without any courses credits, because available places are taken by students from the secondary academic or general stream.

There are a number of steps that can be taken by policy-makers and other stakeholders to encourage improved TVET articulation arrangements:

— Educational programmes should be designed to have clear entry and exit pathways.

— Pathways might provide for a range of outcomes, depending on the type of course and the capacity and inclination of the individual. A technical college, polytechnic or community college graduate might advance to further studies within a TVET institution, transfer to a university or similar institution or undertake further training on the job. All learners should have the option of going further, commensurate with their abilities and the demands of the job market.

— A national qualifications framework which spans TVET and university-level qualifications should be established. Such a framework will enhance the status of TVET because it will act to clarify the standing of programmes and foster recognition and transferability.

— If institutional bottlenecks occur which limit realistic articulation arrangements for TVET programme graduates, alternative delivery arrangements could be structured to meet demand. For example, open and distance learning (ODL) delivery could extend programmes to student groups that are excluded because of quotas, the constraints of employment or geographic location. Increasingly, the potential for programme delivery using the Internet and other flexible delivery mechanisms will make it possible to cater to students who are currently beyond the reach of educational institutions.

— Post-secondary institutions should be encouraged to codify credit transfer and recognise prior learning arrangements. This will help create an environment where articulation practices are the norm.

— Where appropriate, bridging programmes to facilitate articulation can be created.

— Frequently articulation arrangements are poor because there is a lack of continuity between programmes. Carefully constructed bridging or conversion programmes might conveniently and economically be delivered through ODL. They might also be built on knowledge and abilities already attained, and address any deficiencies. For example, a polytechnic diploma graduate may desire to articulate to a related university degree, but be refused admission on the basis of shortcomings in mathematics and science. A specially designed bridging programme should be capable of addressing such difficulties.

— Co-operation on curriculum design should be encouraged. It may, in many instances, be possible for TVET institutions and universities to collaborate when making changes to curriculum so that there is more synergy between related programmes. Not only can such co-operation make articulation more effective, but in some instances credit transfer arrangements might also be enhanced. However, collaboration should not be at the expense of the overall objectives of any programme. If such an outcome were to result, it is likely that the standing of courses could be compromised, with the inevitable adverse reaction by stakeholders.

— Where entry to university ordinarily favours school leavers selected from the academic stream of secondary school, there could be a modest quota made available for the entry of TVET programme graduates based on merit. This may be a very difficult matter for developing countries to address when available funds to support education tend to be rationed out, and the perception that less meritoriously qualified applicants were being given preferential treatment would need to be worked through.

— In some countries it may be feasible for private post-secondary institutions to improve articulation possibilities by making available places that are unavailable in government-funded institutions. Moves in this direction should take place within the umbrella of a national qualifications framework and quality-control systems so that, regardless of the funding arrangements used to support educational institutions, a consistent process exists to ensure a satisfactory outcome.

India: Unresolved Constraints to Articulation

Although India is approaching universal provision of elementary education, the broad provision of secondary education is still an objective to be attained, but secondary participation is growing and is a high national priority. Within the current secondary education system at years 11 and 12 is located the Vocational Education Program (VEP), which is the vocational stream of upper secondary school and which runs in parallel to the academic stream. It is the largest TVET programme in India. Around 30% of VEP graduates enter the job market within two to three years of graduation.

However, experience has demonstrated that many students seek to proceed to further studies, especially to degree level at a university or a diploma at a polytechnic. In practice, however, effective pathways out of the VEP have proved difficult. Students coming from the academic stream get preference for admission to university and polytechnics because they better satisfy the entry requirements, which are set by individual institutions. Despite national policy providing that graduates of vocational courses should be given opportunities for professional growth and career improvement through bridging arrangements, this has not been acted on broadly. The whole question of articulated pathways for VEP graduates has been the subject of considerable debate in India since the early 1980s. There has been considerable pressure from students, parents and educators to improve arrangements.

Some universities have moved to provide vocational subjects within their undergraduate degree programmes, but these subjects are not well connected to the studies in the VEP at this juncture. The use of flexible learning institutions, such as the Indira Ghandi National Open University (IGNOU) to assist in providing studies is seen as having great potential to address this demand. Clearly, the need for articulation in India is now well recognised and relevant policy is being debated. Changes to the economy and developments from the expansion of demand for secondary education may provide incentive for further refinement of articulation arrangements.

Articulation Arrangements

Technical and vocational education (TVE) courses in a number of countries in the South East Asian region. Particular reference is made to Australia, Indonesia, Malaysia, the Philippines, Singapore and Thailand. The countries selected were representative of states at varying degrees of evolution as regards their educational development. Australia being at the edge of the South East Asian region, was included as an example of a country having an interesting history of articulation practices.

Technical and vocational education (TVE) will be regarded as also encompassing technical and vocational education and training (TVET). TVE is usually seen as having a focus on formal programs of study resulting in an academic award, (usually a Certificate or Diploma). Vocational training is normally directed at short term development of specific skills. In practice, there is usually some overlap between vocational education and training, and TVE courses will generally incorporate significant exposure to relevant skills training.

The key feature of articulation in an educational sense is the existence of pathways which allow graduates of one course of study to progress, or 'articulate', to another. Articulation is usually thought of in a context of provision of pathways 'upwards', especially from TVE to university, but 'reverse articulation' also applies to traffic between higher education and TVE. The possibility of articulation arrangements between related courses at the same level, is a further example of educational articulation, but may not be perceived as such. Articulation is important because it is related to opportunity. Articulation is related to status, because 'dead end' courses which do not have pathways to further study opportunities, have less status than programs which do provide further options. Articulation is significant on the broader scale, and at the national level. Nations which have structured or encouraged their educational system to provide effective articulation arrangements, are better placed to capitalize on opportunities that advance economic growth, particularly when technological change or other forces demand a response. A workforce educated in an open ended system will more easily make the transition to new types of employment as they emerge.

All countries which are the subject of this study have some provision for articulation from TVE programs, although such provision is sometimes limited in scope. Credit transfer arrangements through the granting of course credits for recognized studies previously undertaken, are frequently an important facet of articulation arrangements. Credit transfer may occur when institutions agree to formally recognize studies undertaken by students in a sending institution, with the granting of an agreed amount of credit in a particular course, or courses, by the receiving institution. Recognition of prior learning, may be granted to an individual seeking advanced standing in a course. Such recognition may be accorded on the basis of previous studies, or non-formal learning gained through a variety of means, or be a mixture of formal and non-formal learning. In the South East Asian region, the concept of recognition of prior learning has not been widely applied to the granting of advanced standing in formal courses. The desirability of making provision for TVE students who have the ability to undertake further studies is by no means new. For example, the 1964 UNESCO/ILO statement on Technical and Vocational Education and Training contended that , 'Technical and vocational education should be so organised that every person can continue his education until his potentialities have been developed'.

National need and individual aspirations

Countries of this type require an adaptable well educated workforce, and widespread opportunity for further study, simply to maintain their position. In such an environment an individual will be encouraged to undertake further education or training, perhaps in response to a desired career change, or enforced by redundancy brought about by technological change which in turn produces obsolescence of vocational skills. It is not so much a question of having an expectation that TVE courses should be designed with the view that graduates might have the option to go on and undertake related higher level studies, but that TVE programs must be vocational. Their function is to deliver personnel able to undertake skilled work, and create a body of proficient technicians and technologists, but should not be so limited. Intertwined with these objectives, TVE courses should be structured to permit those who have the capacity, to undertake further studies aided by their TVE experience.

Many countries in the South East Asian region have had, until recently, economies based on agrarian and extractive industries. Some countries in the region, have in past decades, been subject to the effects of war and its aftermath, political or economic turmoil, or other disruption which has resulted economic dislocation and restricted the ability of governments' to encourage the broad provision of education. Only recently have many countries been able to provide universal primary education. The provision of secondary education, or partial secondary education is still limited in some countries, particularly in rural areas and, in some cases limited by gender. Associated with the desirability of broad provision of articulation, is the necessity of providing basic education at the primary and secondary level that is broad in nature, and results in students graduating not only with good levels of literacy and numeracy, but also with the knowledge and ability to adapt to developing circumstances. For many countries in the region, a significant focus of TVE provision is at the secondary level. The general availability of postsecondary technical and vocational education and higher education is something that many countries will struggle to provide for decades.

A criticism made from time to time is that TVE programs can be too specialized, and directed at skills training, such skills often having little relevance to industrial needs, and personnel so trained being less adaptable than those who have undertaken education programs of a general nature. Another way of looking at this problem is that it is desirable for formal TVE courses to have as a core general aspects of education and to avoid early specialization. It would be desirable if secondary education was general in nature to leave open further options, such as some provision of vocational education subjects.

For many countries in the region, such an objective is constrained by limited funds. As it will probably be difficult to make secondary education universally available for some time, there is pressure in a number of countries in the region to provide at least some skills training for those who will, for economic or other reasons, be obliged to terminate their studies in the early years of secondary school. In the period up to the 1980s, the World Bank was a major supporter of technical education. In recent times, the Bank has expressed a preference for broad academic secondary courses, rather than courses with a vocational bias. The economic value of vocational education has been questioned. Improved training programs in both the private and government sectors, are now promoted by the Bank, directed at immediate industrial need and following broad academic preparation. Complicating the provision of training in many countries is the somewhat fragmented nature of responsibility for program delivery which may be spread between formal and non-formal, government, private and industry based training providers.

The economies of many countries in the South East Asian region have a large demand for unskilled and semi-skilled workers, and this is likely to continue. Indeed many economies are driven by the need to provide employment for those who have low levels of education and related skills. Such workers receive low wages, and if subject to higher levels of pay, then industries based on this arrangement might become uncompetitive and migrate to lower wage countries. Nevertheless, without the ready availability of well educated and adaptable personnel at all levels of a workforce, it is difficult for advance to higher levels of prosperity.

Change of postsecondary education

Throughout the region the trend is for primary education to be universally available. The region have as an objective the provision of secondary education for as many young people as possible. A longer term issue is the changing nature of postsecondary education. The time will come when some form of mass postsecondary education will tend to become universal, particularly as national economies develop industrially. At present, the postsecondary provision of TVE is usually seen as being a quite different form of education to that provided by universities. It may be that the nature of work in the future will result in more convergence between postsecondary TVE and university education, as the need for education that leaves open future options, particularly at the lower levels of postsecondary education, becomes more widespread.

Driving such a trend might be the lessening of emphasis on skills development in formal courses, towards a broad demand for adaptable graduates; who might be able to quickly acquire specific skills as necessary. Such a concept may currently seem of limited relevance to many economies in South East Asia, but given the pace of change the emergence of such a trend may well occur sooner rather than later. The 1996 UNESCO Delors Report picks up the notion of a broader role for higher education , seeing as important that universities should extend their reach as broadly as possible, 'to be places of culture and learning open to all, (and in a position to provide)—learning throughout life'. Interestingly, the 1994 International Bank for Reconstruction and Development report Higher Education—The Lessons of Experience took the view that non-universities in both the government and private sectors, had an important part to play in the provision of postsecondary vocational education, with scope for articulation arrangements.

Information technology educational implications

Advances in computer based learning and delivery systems, as well as and the steady decline in the cost of such arrangements increasingly will provide long term opportunities to increase the broad provision of postsecondary education. Information technology has considerable scope to enhance the possibility of TVE graduates, and others, to undertake at least part of their studies at a place and time that meets individual need. This is an important consideration for individuals living in remote locations that do not have relevant educational institutions, or in one of the many congested cities where even getting from home to work is a slow, time consuming daily chore.

The role of private education

It is important to take cognizance of the role of non-government or privately funded education institutions in many countries of South East Asian region. Privately funded educational institutions play a vital role, not only at the primary and secondary level, but also in the provision of technical and vocational education, and higher education. The role of the private sector in the provision of postsecondary education is often overlooked, but this sector is frequently the largest provider of postsecondary education in a country eg. Indonesia and the Philippines. The pressure for places in government funded universities in many South East Asian countries, has resulted in only the most academically gifted students gaining entry. In such an environment the possibility of articulation between TVE and university is very limited. In these circumstances articulation options may be more likely to occur in the private sector of education.

The international dimension of articulation

The fee paying option has been extended in recent years to the international sphere. It has become common for those secondary school and TVE course graduates in the South East Asian region who are unable to gain entry to a university, to look abroad for a place as an international fee paying student. This option has been a function of rising income levels in the region, but recent economic disturbances have tended to check this trend. Currently, popular destinations for international study are Europe, North America and Australasia. As the quality of education improves in some South East Asian countries, it is probable that the intercontinental nature of articulation arrangements will expand to include significant intercountry movement of students in search of further education, and some countries in the region are moving to accommodate this demand.

Scant published material exists on the topic of educational articulation for most countries subject to this study. As a result an important source of information was to interview a number of individuals who had significant involvement in the field of education, and in particular TVE, and higher education. Some attempts were made to ascertain the views of representatives of industry and commerce, regarding the desirability of articulation pathways as the norm in the national provision of education, but this aspect of the study was limited, and might well be followed up by further research.

What follows is consideration of the question of articulation arrangements for TVE students in the South East Asian region, on a country by country basis. This review is against the background of the economic development in each country and the general system of education, with particular reference paid to the provision of TVE. Since commencing this study, most countries in the South East Asian region have been subject to serious economic disturbance, the full impact of which is yet to work through national economies. What effect this will have on national systems of education is yet to be seen. However, serious calamities of this nature frequently act as a catalyst for reflection and subsequent change.

Australia

The Commonwealth of Australia has a land area of about 7 million square km, and climatic regions ranging from tropical in the north to temperate in the south. Australia has a population of about 18.1 million people. Most of the population, together with agricultural activities and centres of manufacturing, are concentrated in the coastal strip along the east coast and south west coastal regions of continental Australia. Although Australia is a substantial exporter of agricultural produce and minerals these sectors of the economy provide limited and generally declining employment opportunities. Manufacturing and construction are significant sectors of the Australian economy, but most employment growth is in the provision of services.

In Australia, the primary/secondary system of education is based on a 6 + 6 year cycle of schooling. Few barriers exist to prevent students completing 12 years of schooling. Attendance at school is compulsory from 6 until at least 15 years of age. For school leavers, entry to university undergraduate degree programs is based on performance in the relevant senior secondary (year 12) certificate course. In former times, a number of Australian states provided secondary technical education in technical schools, that operated in parallel with more academic secondary high schools. This model of secondary education has been replaced in Australia, with secondary education courses which are general in nature. To cater for a broad spectrum of student ability and interest, a recent trend in Australia has been to permit senior secondary students to undertake some vocational studies, which may be cross credited to vocational education qualifications. This trend is driven by attempts to improve the transition between school and employment, particularly for those students who do not wish to proceed to university at this stage. There are 37 government funded universities in Australia, and two private universities. The small number of private universities is partly a reflection of the fact that places in undergraduate courses at government funded universities were provided on the basis that cost of tuition was largely paid by the Australian Government.

Technical and vocational education

In Australia, technical and vocational education is frequently referred to as vocational education and training (VET). In broad terms, vocational education and training covers preparation and ongoing retraining, for a broad sweep of occupations, ranging from the operative through to the para-professional level. The delivery of formal VET programs in Australia has, until recently, mainly been the responsibility of government funded technical and further education (TAFE) colleges. These efforts were supplemented by the training colleges of government bodies, the armed services and to a lesser extent private educational providers. In addition, there is a well established provision of informal education and training in Australia, mainly directed at adult and community education, but often providing elements of what might be considered vocational education. Over the last decade successive Australian Governments have encouraged much broader provision of vocational education and training through government and non-government providers, including TAFE colleges/ institutes, private colleges, industry training centres, group training schemes, and in-house training arrangements. There are about 80 TAFE institutes in Australia with many operating on a multi-campus basis. Some universities also provide VET courses, mainly at the paraprofessional level. To facilitate broader provision of vocational education and training in Australia, a number of steps have been taken to establish a more open training market which is driven by demand rather than input of resources, including:

Establishment of a framework for qualifications, standards and assessment which apply to both government and non-government providers of vocational education and training. Transferability of recognition of formal education and training between providers. Encouragement of competition between government and non-government vocational education and training providers. This is enhanced by government funding assistance for some programs provided by non-government providers. A focus on competency based training directed at the needs of industry and commerce, with a shift away from time-dependant programs. Mechanisms for recognition of prior learning gained by individuals through formal or informal means.

Establishment of the industry based Australian National Training Authority (ANTA) in 1994, to formulate national strategic plans and objectives for the provision of VET. The Australian Qualifications Framework which was introduced in 1995, encompasses vocational education and training awards, as well as higher education courses delivered by universities. This framework of qualifications replaced all former certificates, advanced certificates and associate diplomas awarded by vocational education and training providers in Australia.

Secondary students have the option of leaving school after about year 10, and might at that time commence an apprenticeship or traineeship. In recent years, under the Australian Traineeship system, the notion of an apprenticeship has been extended beyond what were previously considered to be traditional trade occupations. During an apprenticeship/traineeship period a student works through a training program leading to certificates I - IV. These studies generally articulate to VET diploma/advanced diploma programs. Given the trend for students to complete secondary school, many students enter a TAFE college, or another VET provider, and undertake a post year 12 diploma/ advanced diploma course. A diploma/advanced diploma would require normally 2-3 years of full-time studies, or perhaps be a combination of part-time/full-time studies over a longer period.

Articulation

In the decades prior to the 1960s it was quite common for senior technical college students in a number of states to undertake a certificate course which articulated to a professional diploma program. In a number of instances, cooperative arrangements existed which permitted technical college diploma graduates of demonstrated ability to articulate to related university degree programs, with advanced standing. These practices were disturbed in the 1960s when senior technical colleges in Australia were removed from the technical college system in each state, and redesignated what at the time were known as 'colleges of advanced education' (CAEs). CAEs were established to provide tertiary level studies of a more applied nature than were delivered by universities, and were the consequence of an investigation into the national provision of higher education by the 1964 Martin Committee. Initial CAE course offerings did not extend beyond the professional diploma courses previously conducted by the technical colleges. However, by the early 1970s the CAEs, which later absorbed many former teacher training colleges, had moved to introduce degree level programs. During the early 1990s, the CAEs underwent a further metamorphosis to become universities in their own right, or were absorbed by existing universities as a consequence of decisions by the Australian Government which required rationalization and consolidation of the higher education sector. What remained of the technical college system in Australia at the postsecondary level was reworked into what became TAFE colleges during the 1970s.

During the 1960s, when diploma courses were transferred from technical colleges to the CAEs, concerns were raised by a number of parties including trade unions and educators, regarding the loss of convenient linkages between vocational and higher education courses. Students wishing to articulate between vocational and higher education programs during this era were subject to assessment on a case by case basis, which proved to be somewhat inconsistent. During the 1980s the efficacy of articulation arrangements for TAFE course graduates began to be questioned, and has subsequently led to a more open approach, which was the result of a number of factors including:

— The number of TAFE college graduates from paraprofessional courses that subsequently sought higher level studies increased significantly.

— The provision of TAFE courses was greatly improved both in terms of course delivery resourcing, quality and availability during the 1970s, in the wake of higher levels of government funding.

— The entry level to higher level TAFE courses gradually increased until completion of secondary education became the norm for many courses.

— Technological change impacting on industry and commerce encouraged the existing workforce to undertake further studies, not necessarily in a field of previous study.

— Social pressure, exemplified by trade union calls for removal of artificial barriers to further study became stronger.

Government at the national level, gradually became more interested in seeking ways to improve articulation arrangements, for a number of reasons including social justice for disadvantaged groups, and the need to improve the provision of education to enhance economic growth. State educational authorities became more sensitive of the need to improve linkages between vocational education programs under their control, as well as linkages between TAFE and related higher education institutions. The 1985 report Articulation of TAFE Middle-Level and Higher Education Courses in Australia, by the TAFE National Centre for Research and Development chronicles the limited opportunities and difficulties faced by TAFE course graduates wishing to articulate to higher level studies at that time.

In 1989, the Australian Government in the White Paper, Higher Education, A Policy Statement, documented its concerns on the somewhat ad hoc credit transfer arrangements between TAFE and higher education and set out a number of principles that it expected higher education institutions to adopt, including:

— Transferring students should receive maximum possible credit for completed work.

— There should be continuing dialogue between higher education and TAFE institutions to establish means by which cooperative planning of TAFE courses, may facilitate credit transfer.

— Individual institutions should codify and publish information on the extent of credit which they are prepared to grant in recognition of work done in other institutions.

— Arrangements should be available so that students who believe that their previous academic study justifies exemption from particular units may have credit transfer decisions reviewed.

Many factors have created a climate which has encouraged improvements to articulation arrangements for vocational education students to undertake higher level studies, and in 1993, at least 8.3% of all students who university courses in Australia had commenced or completed a VET course. Information about pathways through postsecondary education courses is more widespread and routinely appears in TAFE college and university handbooks. Secondary students are made aware of the education pathways open to them. Higher education staff involved in the enrolment process have become familiar with the notion of articulation and where applicable credit transfer arrangements. It has became commonplace for the accreditation process in both VET and higher education, for course approval submissions to demonstrate a clear indication of articulation pathways. This concept has been taken up by the Institution of Engineers Australia as part of its course recognition process which now requires articulation arrangements to be described in all courses submitted to it for recognition and assessment.

A small number of 'dual sector' educational institutions exist in Australia that have both VET and higher education components. These institutions are Swinburne University of Technology, RMIT University, Victoria University of Technology (all in Victoria), the Australian Maritime College in Tasmania, and the Northern Territory University. These institutions have developed comprehensive policies to enhance articulation arrangements. Recently, the Victorian Government announced that a number of TAFE colleges will amalgamate with universities, in part to further improve articulation arrangements.

Higher education programs offered through the distance education mode provide significant articulation opportunities for VET course graduates, particularly those in remote geographic locations, or those who otherwise find it difficult for various reasons to attend classes. Generally, courses offered through off-campus studies have the same entry requirements and course credit arrangements that apply in respect of courses conducted on-campus, including allowances made for the entry of mature age applicants to courses. In many cases students can enrol in single subjects without prerequisites.

In Australia there is widespread articulation of individuals from the university sector to vocational education programs at TAFE colleges. This might be described as 'reverse articulation'. The two-way nature of articulation between VET and higher education in Australia, is such that there is now more traffic between higher education and VET than the other way round. Not only that, there is evidence indicating that articulation is a multidirectional phenomenon with more than half the students who migrate between vocational education and the university sectors previously enrolled in more than one tertiary course. Whereas there has been considerable dialogue over decades to bring about improvements in articulation arrangements between VET and higher education by those having an interest in this matter, 'reverse articulation' is a phenomenon which has grown without any perceived encouragement by government, educational authorities or institutions. Demand has been a function of individual need.

What is apparent in Australia is that there is now considerable community pressure for widespread provision of postsecondary education, in contrast to the situation which applied in former times when postsecondary education was seen as only being necessary for small numbers of people. The 1998 West Committee felt it necessary to comment on this matter with the statement that the 'national target should be near universal access to some form of postsecondary education'. Given increasing pressure for individuals to undertake further education and training simply to cope with change it is apparent that the pressure to continue improvements of articulation arrangements in Australia will increase.

Indonesia

The Republic of Indonesia consists of more than 13,000 islands, with a population of about 195 million. The island of Java, is densely populated with about 60% of the national population, and contains the largest cities in Indonesia. The capital Jakarta has a population exceeding 15 million people.

About 50% of the population of Indonesia is still engaged in agriculture. Manufacturing and the provision of services have been sectors of the economy demonstrating increasing growth. However, recent economic disturbances have seriously effected the financial stability of Indonesia. Manufacturing sectors include textiles, clothing and footwear, food processing, electrical/electronics, automotive, pulp and paper, and chemicals.

Indonesia has a system of primary/secondary education based on 6 years of primary education, followed by 3 years of junior secondary education and 3 years of senior secondary education. Primary education is tending towards universal provision, although in some remote areas not all students complete 6 years of education. Efforts are being made to extend the compulsory attendance of children at school through to year 9. Currently about 45% of children aged 13 - 15 years attend junior secondary school. Education at senior secondary school is provided through the following types of school:

— Academic Senior Secondary School (SMU)

— Technical/Vocational Senior Secondary School (SMK)

— Madrasha (Islamic) School

Academic senior secondary schools provide a 3 year curriculum which leads towards entry to a higher education institution. The majority of students entering senior secondary schooling opt for this type of education in preference to the offerings of the technical/vocational senior secondary school. Technical/vocational senior secondary schools are seen as leading directly to the world of work, and offer 3 year programs intended to produce graduates to serve the needs of Indonesian industry at the skilled worker level. Schools of this type tend to specialize in particular vocational areas such as economics and business, engineering, agriculture, art and craft, building, etc. In 1996, there were about 3000 private and 700 government senior secondary technical/ vocational schools. Enrolments in these institutions was about 1 million in private schools and 500,000 in government schools.

Although senior secondary technical/vocational education schools were seen as providing a steady stream of skilled workers for the Indonesian workforce, it has been found that only about 20% of graduates proceed to employment. There is a reluctance of parents to place children in secondary technical schools.

Higher education in Indonesia at undergraduate degree level and above is delivered through universities, institutes and (tertiary) schools. In addition, there exists the publicly funded Universitas Terbuka (Open University). Private provision of education is significant at all levels in Indonesia, particularly at the secondary and postsecondary levels. Indeed most postsecondary education is provided by private educational institutions.

Private postsecondary education has a very long history in Indonesia, extending back to the period of

Dutch colonial administration. Encouragement for private education grew in the post independence period, and since the 1950s has undergone significant growth. Many public universities and institutes that have emerged in Indonesia have had their roots in private colleges, which have subsequently been taken over by the state.

Postsecondary Technical and Vocational Education

Indonesian postsecondary technical and vocational education is delivered through a number of educational bodies including universities.

— *Diploma courses:* Full-time diploma programs up to 4 years in duration, are offered through polytechnics, some universities, institutes and academies. Courses offered at the diploma level include studies in engineering, business studies, tourism, forestry, etc.

Indonesian diploma granting entities differ in terms of their structure and awards:

— Academies are single faculty institutions - Diploma programs.

— Polytechnics are multi faculty institutions - Diploma programs.

— Schools often only one faculty - Diplomas and some undergraduate degrees (S1) Institutes have university level status - Diplomas and undergraduate degrees.

— Universities - Diplomas and degrees to PhD.

Diploma level courses are seen as being applicable for occupations at the advanced technician level. Diploma courses have a vocational rather than an academic focus and are designed to be terminal in nature, leading directly to employment. Entrants to diploma level courses are overwhelmingly graduates from academic senior secondary schools, although it is possible for those from technical/vocational senior secondary schools to gain entry.

— *Other programmes:* Also included in the category of postsecondary programs might be the non-formal programs of vocational and skills training provided by government and private entities, and industry training centres. Students at such centres may not have completed their secondary schooling, but have left school.

The Ministry of Labour and Social Welfare, through the Department of Manpower Training has 31 (BLK) Worker Training Centres offering a variety of programs:

— Initial Training Programs (1 year)

— Single skill training (2-3 months)

— Multiskill training integrated (3 years)

— Short upgrading programs (8)

Groups of medium sized companies have combined to establish group training units (CGTU). Up to 40 companies are served by each CGTU. The role of private Indonesian training colleges is most significant. These offer a wide variety of short and medium term training courses. Private training colleges are closely attuned to the employment market and offer courses in response to demand. It is noted that about 20,000 such institutions exist and range from small shop-front centres to substantial urban institutions. It has been estimated that about 4.5 million students annually enrol in programs provided by private training colleges, and this sector has experienced strong growth.

The scope for articulation of technical and vocational education students in Indonesia is significant but its practicalities are complicated, and not easily implemented on a wide scale at this time. Entry to government university undergraduate degree courses from technical/vocational senior secondary schools is not possible, and reflects the intense pressure for places, which go to the most able students from academic stream senior secondary school graduates.

The possibility of entry to a government polytechnic diploma increases somewhat, but even here students from academic senior high schools tend to get more offers for placement. It appears that this is currently being looked at and may result in some modifications to the technical/vocational senior secondary school courses, possibly a bridging program for those desirous of entering a polytechnic. Generally, there is little scope for a polytechnic diploma graduate to articulate to a degree program at a government university, although this is looked at on a case by case basis. The numbers of students using this route is understood to be very small. There are some exceptions to this situation. If a student has the means, it is possible for students to circumvent the limited funded places at some government universities, including Universitus Indonesia (University of Indonesia), and gain entry to degree courses via fee paying extension programs. Extension programs are available to both school leavers and mature age students.

The situation in the private education sector is somewhat different. Some Indonesian private vocational colleges have links with private universities. If a graduate from a private vocational college has the ability, and the financial means, articulation/entry to a private university is possible. The necessity to extend the availability of secondary and tertiary education in Indonesia is very great, but the resources to permit this to occur are limited, providing significant support of private education. The need to improve the quality of education is also a matter for debate in Indonesia and is cause for priority consideration.

Technical and vocational education is under significant pressure to improve the relevance of courses. The then Minister of Education and Culture, encouraged greater links between education and the world of work, particularly at the senior secondary level. There is an awareness that future planning will require an education and training system that is more directed at the ongoing needs of industry and commerce, by way of flexibility of multiple entry and exit points.

Malaysia

Malaysia has a public system of education which provides 6 years of primary education, followed by 5 years of secondary education. However, students from Chinese and Tamil medium schools, are required to undertake an additional year of study after the completion of primary school, which is aimed at improving competency in the national language Bahasa Melayu. At the end of three years of the lower secondary school program, students undertake an examination, the Penilaian Menengah Rendah (PMR). Entry to upper secondary school programs is based on PMR results. At this point the less able student might leave the formal education system. Education in upper secondary school is delivered in the following types of school:

— Normal Academic Schools

— Secondary Technical Schools

— Secondary Vocational Schools

Students undertaking the academic stream complete a 2 year course leading to the Sijil Pelajaran Malaysia (SPM) (Malaysian Certificate of Education) examination. A satisfactory SPM result permits entry to a 2 year pre-university program, which concludes with the Sijil Tinggi Pereskolahan Malaysia (SPTM) (Malaysian Higher School Certificate) examination. Secondary technical schools, also provide the 4 year SPM/SPTM program which includes vocational and technology electives, in engineering, commerce, home economics and agricultural science. The secondary vocational school, offers 2 year programs designed to provide an entry to paid employment. The course has an academic core, and vocational studies comprise about 50% of the program. Successful completion of this course results in the award of the Sijil Pelajaran Malaysia Vokasional (SPMV) (Malaysian Certificate of Education Vocational). Although the SPMV has a vocational focus, there are nevertheless articulation pathways for further study open to SPMV graduates. There is also a extensive network of private primary and secondary schools. These institutions which are open to all Malaysian citizens, follow the national curriculum and examinations.

It should be noted that the Malaysian Government is moving to change the 6+5+2 year cycle of primary/ secondary education, to 6+4+2 year cycle with 4 years of secondary education followed by 2 years of pre-university studies. In addition to extensive provision of TVE in Malaysia, there are eight government universities.

A significant reason for improving the Malaysian system of education is a long term Malaysian Government objective to make Malaysia an important regional centre for the provision of education.

Postsecondary technical and vocational education

Postsecondary technical and vocational education in Malaysia is provided by a mix of public and private institutions, including:

— Government polytechnics, some universities and institutes, skills training centres, and a number of ministries.

— Private colleges described variously as schools, colleges, institutes, institutes of technology and academies.

These entities are classified as Private Higher Educational Institutions (PHEIs). Skills training is also encouraged under the Seventh Malaysia Plan which recognizes the need to improve Malaysia's human resource as a key factor in national economic growth. Assistance for skill training is provided under the Human Resources Development Fund (HRDF) which makes significant contributions towards the cost of training at government and private training centres.

Considerable training activity takes place with HRDF assistance at the enterprize level. A recent World Bank/Government of Malaysia report investigating key factors of advancing Malaysian industry encouraged the expansion of high quality skills training in the private sector training.

Industrial training institutes

These institutes provide certificate level training programs of 6 months to 2 years duration, and produce skilled workers in the fields of mechanical engineering, electrical, printing and construction. Depending on the program, entry requirements range from PMR to SPM/ SPMV.

National youth training institutes

These institutes offer vocational training to young people in preparation for employment at the skilled worker level. Based on SPM entry, certificate programs are offered in various fields including automotive maintenance, electrical technology, refrigeration, electronics, construction, gardening, textiles, and hospitality. They range in duration from 12 months to 2 years. There are 7 National Youth Training Institutes.

Polytechnics

Polytechnics provide 2 year certificate and 3 year diploma courses in business, engineering, architecture and construction. These programs are directed at students seeking technician and middle management levels. Polytechnic courses are based on SPM/SPMV entry. There are seven government polytechnics.

MARA Institute of Technology (ITM)

A range of 3 year diploma courses are provided in a number of fields including business, applied science, building, interior design, engineering, computer science, tourism and hospitality management. These courses are based on SPM/SPMV entry. ITM also offers 6 month to 1 year certificate courses in hospitality based on PMR entry. ITM limits entry to bumiputra Malaysians, and has 12 campuses.

Universities

Of the eight government universities the Universiti Technologi Malaysia (University of Technology Malaysia) and Universiti Putra Malaysia (University of Putra Malaysia) provide a number of 3 year diploma courses based on SPM entry. A number of Malaysian government agencies other than those listed above also offer TVE courses and skills training programs.

Private TVE institutions

Provision of private postsecondary education in Malaysia is very extensive, having grown significantly over the last decade or so. This growth was encouraged by limited places being available in government postsecondary institutions, particularly universities. Many private colleges have also developed a of range technical and vocational education courses at diploma and certificate level. Technical and vocational education programs offered by Malaysian private colleges (PHEIs), although subject to Ministry of Education approval, do not have to follow government set curriculum. Diploma programs normally require 3 years full time tuition post SPM. Certificate courses tend to vary in length from 6 months to 2 years post SPM. Some courses are structured such that a certificate course feeds into a related diploma course. There are more than 70 significant private colleges in Malaysia, and further growth in this sector is anticipated. The expansion of private institutions has emerged from a government stance of firm containment during the 1970s, to that of controlled development in recent years.

The Malaysian Government has provided significant encouragement to the private sector to establish technical and vocational colleges through generous taxation concessions and legislative support which permit the establishment of such institutions. Hundreds of private sector training institutions also provide skills training programs.

Some private training institutions are also private higher education institutions eg. Federal Institute of Technology, Informatics College, Workers Institute of Technology, Kolej TAFE, and the Malaysian Institute of Management. For a training activity to receive support under the Human Resources Development Fund the training program must be approved by the Human Resources Development Council.

Although Malaysian universities are under considerable pressure to accept only the best SPTM graduates into undergraduate programs, there is some provision for those who complete polytechnic diplomas with merit to undertake higher level studies. For example, the Universiti Malaya (University of Malaya) will consider graduates holding relevant polytechnic diplomas for entry to undergraduate degrees in a number of fields including engineering, computer science, pharmacy and law. Likewise entry to a number of Mara Institute of Technology degree programs is based on completion of a related ITM diploma or a diploma from another recognized institution. A number of private colleges deliver significant segments of degree courses, under arrangements with foreign universities primarily in the United Kingdom, the United States of America, Canada and Australia. A typical arrangement is that a Malaysian college would effectively deliver the curriculum of the first year or two of the degree course of a foreign university, with the student travelling abroad to the twinned university to complete the course. There are other variations to this model, which include preparation by Malaysian colleges for qualifying examinations of overseas (esp. United Kingdom) professional bodies such as the UK Engineering Council; credit transfer arrangements which allow studies undertaken at a Malaysian private college to be given advanced standing at the counterpart foreign university; or delivery of a distance education course in association with a Malaysian college. An example of such an arrangement are the activities of the Malaysian Institute of Management which offers a wide range of training courses, as well as its own certificates and diplomas, mainly in the field of management. Students who complete an MIM diploma or another relevant diploma are able to undertake studies at MIM whereby they articulate to a number of degree programs including MBAs awarded by the University of Bath (UK), University of Hull (UK), Maastricht School of Management (Netherlands), or RMIT University (Australia).

Graduates of the Workers Institute of Technology 3 year Diplomas of Engineering have the opportunity to proceed to 21 affiliated polytechnics in Britain as well as colleges and universities in Australia. Advanced standing of the Workers Institute of Technology Diplomas have permitted students to gain a degree after two years of additional study. Given the economic difficulties of late, and recognizing the advanced state of private provision of education in Malaysia, the Government has encouraged many private colleges to extend their twinning programs to allow students to complete their degrees in Malaysia. This trend should obviate much of the need for study abroad by Malaysian students.

The structure of articulation arrangements which have been established in Malaysia permits broad opportunities for further educational attainment. In particular, the concept that all levels of education should provide further possibilities for ongoing studies sets the scene for future growth in response to national and individual need.

The Philippines

The Republic of Philippines is an archipelago of more than 7,000 islands, with a population of about 70 million people. In 1995, about 36% of Gross Domestic Product was produced by manufacturing, mining, and construction, the provision of services 43%,. with agriculture responsible for 21% of GDP. The Philippines has a workforce of approximately 29 million. Primary education in the Philippines is based on six years of tuition. Primary education is followed by four years of secondary education. The adult literacy rate is about 94%. Because of financial constraints not all children are able to progress to complete secondary school. Technical education is provided at the secondary level in both government and non-government schools.

Postsecondary technical and vocational education

In the decades prior to 1994, the administration of TVE was the responsibility of several bodies:

— The National Manpower and Youth Council which was established in 1966 to integrate all skills training programs in the Philippines.

— The Bureau of Technical and Vocational Education of the Department of Education, Culture and Sports, which was created in 1985 but grew out of earlier administrative arrangements that managed the provision of technical and vocational education in secondary and postsecondary schools and colleges.

— The Apprenticeship program of the Bureau of Local Employment of the Department of Labour and Employment.

Since 1994, technical and vocational education in the Philippines has been under the supervision of the Technical Education and Skills Development Authority (TESDA). This includes both government and non-government providers of TVE.

The objectives of TESDA are to

— Help the country attain global competitiveness through improved technical education and skills development.

— Focus technical education and skills development on meeting the demand for quality middle-level manpower.

— Enhance workers critical and creative thinking through the dissemination of the scientific and technical base of middle-level manpower development programs.

— Encourage the complementary roles of private and public institutions in technical education and skills development systems.

— Enhance character development of the citizen worker by emphasizing work ethic, · discipline, resourcefulness and nationalism.

Postsecondary TVE programs on offer include 1 - 2 year certificate courses directed at trade/technician education. 3 year diploma courses are also available. Fields of study include agriculture, agro-industry, computing, business and management, health, transport, languages, engineering, police studies and security. Given the influence of the United States in the evolution of education in the Philippines, it is not surprizing that a significant feature of educational provision in the Philippines is the large provision of education by non-government educational institutions. In the technical and vocational education sector the provision of about 30% of TVE institutions are government funded, with the remaining 70% of TVE institutions in the hands of non-government organizations such as corporations, religious bodies, and companies. Higher education institutions have an even higher level of non-government involvement with 950 (80%) of the 1185 higher education institutions in the Philippines being private entities. In 1995, private higher education institutions enrolled 1.3 million of the 1.7 million students in the Philippines.

The growth of private sector education is a reflection of the financial constraints of successive governments, which have come to rely on the private sector to provide the bulk of postsecondary education. An outcome of this environment, is the wide variation of standards, quality of programs and facilities at both TVE institutions and universities, both public and private. The best examples of both systems are very good, but many institutions struggle to deliver quality programs. In spite of growing demands from the Philippines economy graduates frequently find it difficult to obtain employment in the field for which they have been educated. In this environment there are negative perceptions by many young people towards technical and vocational education.

Articulation

As far back as the 1969-70 Programme of the Presidential Commission to Survey Philippines Education noted the need for greater levels of articulation from elementary to secondary education, as well as pathways to higher education and TVE. There are a number of examples where TVE graduates have gone on to undertake higher level studies. Graduates of the 3 year Diploma in Engineering at Don Bosco Technical College, in Mandaluyang City can articulate, with a one year credit, to the BSc Engineering offered by the College. The same graduates might also gain entry with credits to a Degree course at Adamson University in Manila, but would need to pass the Adamson entry examination.

Although there are accommodation limitations it is nevertheless possible for graduates of trade and technician institutes to transfer to programs at the Technological University of the Philippines (TUP) if they are able to pass the entry examination. Many students undertaking higher level courses at the Technological

University of the Philippines have articulated from the TUP 3 year Diploma of Technology. The Diploma of Technology leads to a 3 year full time BSc engineering degree, a 5 semester part time BEng for technician engineers, and a BTech Teacher Education directed at technician course teachers. This arrangement is referred to in the Philippines as an example of a so called 'ladder curriculum'.

Graduates of the 3 year Diploma of Technology in Electrical Engineering at the Meralco Foundation Institute, in Pasig City are able to articulate to the BEng at the Mapua Institute of Technology. Some Meralco graduates have gone on to undertake a BEng at the Technological University of the Philippines. The Polytechnic University of the Philippines has a secondary technical school, which was originally set up to cater for those unable to gain entry to a degree course. Whilst most courses provided by the technical college are designed for those seeking to go directly to employment, the 2 year Office Administration course articulates to the Bachelor of Business offered by the Polytechnic University of the Philippines. At the more prestigious universities the opportunity for TVE graduates in the Philippines to articulate to higher education in such institutions is very limited. For example, the opportunity for TVE students to articulate into the Bachelor of Engineering course at the University of the Philippines Manila is not an issue. There is no space available, all places are taken by secondary school graduates. TESDA is keen to ensure that TVE courses are open ended because of an awareness that terminal courses are of lesser interest to students. Intertwined with the creation of a climate for encouragement of articulation has been positive action by the Philippines Government to encourage credit transfer through the 1996 Executive Order by President Fidel Ramos which provided machinery for issuance of assessments of academic equivalency for prior learning. From investigations undertaken there is significant provision within the Philippines system of education for TVE graduates to articulate to higher level studies. Given the significant provision of postsecondary in the Philippines by the non-government sector, it is anticipated that market pressures will play an important role in creating. demand for articulation pathways.

Singapore

The Republic of Singapore is an island state. The small land area precludes an agricultural sector of any significance. The population of about 3 million is mainly employed in service industries and in particular financial services. The focus of manufacturing in Singapore is directed towards high technology areas including electronics/computing, petroleum refining, industrial chemicals, etc.

Singapore has been able to exploit its geographic location, not only in the provision of transportation services, but also acts as a provider of services to the region. The state of economic growth in Singapore is quite different to that applying in surrounding countries, and this is reflected in a comprehensive system of education. The quality and relevance of education and training in Singapore is considered to be an important factor in the economic growth of Singapore. Of countries in the immediate region, Singapore has the best developed provision of articulation pathways, between the various segments of the education system. Graduates of vocational education, in both technical institutes and polytechnics have significant opportunities for higher level studies.

In Singapore, the primary/secondary system of education is based on a 6 + 4 or 5 year cycle of schooling. The Singapore-Cambridge General Certificate of Education (GCE) Normal (N) level examination is undertaken after four years of secondary education. The GCE O level examination requires another year of study. High achiever students may undertake the four year postprimary express/special stream after which they may sit for the GCE O level examination. Students with high achievement at the GCE O levels may enter a junior college and undertake a two year pre-university program leading to the GCE A level examination. About 80% of GCE O level graduates go on to further study. Approximately 20% of school leavers will transfer to junior college/university, 40% will enter polytechnic diploma courses, and 20% will undertake Institute of Technical Education programs. Those who opt for employment at this stage find widespread provision of in-house training. Singapore has been able to achieve a well balanced and appropriate system of education as a consequence of considered development and implementation of policy. The New Education System in 1980, introduced ability based streaming from primary school. Another driver of education policy was the report of the 1986 Singapore Economic Committee entitled, The Singapore Economy: New Directions, which made a number of recommendations including:

— Upgrading the median level of education of the Singaporean workforce.

— Provision of ongoing training and retraining for the workforce.

— Expanding and improving all levels of postsecondary education.

Over the last decade these objectives have been met with great success.

Technical and vocational education

Those students who do not gain a place in a junior college have a number of options available for further study at government polytechnics, private postsecondary institutions, the Institute of Technical Education and other entities.

Polytechnics

Singapore has four well equipped government funded polytechnics that offer 3 year diploma courses in a wide spectrum of disciplines including business studies, information technology, engineering, biotechnology, interior design, multimedia, nursing and shipbuilding. Entry to polytechnic diploma courses is based on completion of the GCE O level certificate. Students with GCE A level may enter the second year of diploma programs.

Institute of Technical Education

The Institute of Technical Education (ITE) is a multicampus government institution that offers a wide range of vocational certificate courses to school leavers and working adults. ITE is also the skills standards certification authority for Singapore. Courses provided by ITE include studies in automation, automotive, business studies, building services, electrical, electronics, mechanical, precision engineering, and travel services. Most full time courses are of 2 years duration. Entry to ITE courses caters for both GCE N and O levels graduates. Apprenticeship training is an important facet of ITE activity with 48 apprenticeship programs being offered. Early school leavers with no formal qualifications are catered for through basic vocational training programs. Other facets of ITE include a Basic Education for Skills Training (BEST) program for working adults which provides basic literacy and numeracy courses, and the Worker Improvement through Secondary Education (WISE) program for adults to improve their competency in English and mathematics to GCE N level.

These programs are offered to improve the workforce skill and productivity capability. ITE also offers basic skills training to working adults through several programs including a six month part-time Modular Skills Training (MOST) program for working adults, an Adult Cooperative Training Scheme (ACTS) scheme directed at workers aged between 20 and 40 years of age and conducted in the apprenticeship format, and a Training Initiative for Mature Employees (TIME) modular training program for adults over 40 years of age. The ACTS and TIME programs may be undertaken in English, Mandarin, Malay or Tamil. ITE programs have been designed so that they are interlinked and provide the opportunity for articulation to higher level courses.

LaSalle SIA College of the Arts

Offers 3 year diploma courses based on completion of CGE O level, in fine arts, design, multimedia arts, drama, dance and music. Part-time students are also able to undertake the diploma courses.

SHATEC

The Singapore Hotel Association Training and Education Centre (SHATEC) which is under the control of the Singapore Hotel Association offers a number of diploma and skilled worker training courses for the hospitality and tourism industry.

Singapore Institute of Management

The Singapore Institute of Management (SIM), which is a professional body offers a range of certificate and diploma courses, mainly in the field of management.

Private business and computer colleges

There are a significant number of private colleges in Singapore that offer courses in secretarial training and office administration, computing and business studies.

The Singapore system of education in clearly focused on the world of work, and is continually evolving to assist the upgrading of workforce skills at all levels, to meet both the immediate and long term needs of the Singapore economy and social objectives. As a consequence, the notion of articulation to further programs of study is well entrenched, reflecting the needs of individuals to advance to higher levels of academic attainment, and other forms of education as they progress through their career. This situation has evolved over several decades and reflects the mature nature of the Singaporean economy which is heavily dependant on high technology industries and the provision of services, which in turn encourages upgrading workforce capability.

The compact geographic nature of Singapore, coupled with an excellent public transport infrastructure, has assisted in making it possible for working students to integrate work and further study, something that is quite difficult in a number of other countries in the region. In addition, opportunities exist for participation in flexible course delivery arrangements. There are many opportunities for further study for TVE graduates from Singaporean polytechnics, the Institute of Technical Education, and other bodies. Singapore polytechnics will admit ITE graduates to diploma programs related to their ITE studies. Admission is based on meritorious ITE results. Depending on the level reached in an ITE program, it is possible for advanced standing to courses in some cases. For example, an ITE graduate with a 2 year Certificate in Business Studies post GCE O level, could be offered entry to the second year of a related polytechnic diploma.

Polytechnics in Singapore offer a range of advanced diploma courses. Entry to these courses are based on completion of a related diploma course. Advanced diploma courses are usually offered on a part-time basis over two years and are available in a number of fields including computer & communication systems, multimedia, building services, management, mechatronics, food technology, nursing specialisations and contract administration. Advanced diplomas were developed originally in response to a demand for further education from diploma graduates who desired higher level studies in a particular field. The polytechnics also have strong involvement in continuing education by the provision of short courses, which are directed at upgrading of those currently in the workforce. ITE also provide customised and short skills courses.

The National University of Singapore (NUS) and the Nanyang Technological University (NTU) both admit limited numbers of polytechnic diploma graduates to degree courses with advanced standing where appropriate. For example, the NUS accepts about 300 graduates from polytechnics each year, with 70 odd entering undergraduate courses in engineering, and around 200 being admitted to science and computer programs. The NUS also offers part-time Bachelor of Technology courses specifically directed at polytechnic diploma graduates, to increase the stock of engineers with shopfloor experience to cope with duties of a higher technological nature. About 80 students are enrolled in this course each year.

In addition to offering courses at the certificate and diploma level the Singapore Institute of Management has number of linkages with international universities to deliver selected programs at undergraduate degree, master and doctoral levels, in a number of fields including business, management, economics, mass communications, nursing, education, banking and finance. SIM's international partners include the University of Strathclyde, University of Bradford,

University of London, Nottingham Trent University and Henley Management College (UK), Syracuse University, George Washington University, Rutgers University, and State University of New York at Buffalo (USA), Monash University, RMIT University and the University of Sydney (Australia). A typical arrangement for entry into most undergraduate degree courses, with advanced standing, is that entry is based on completion of a polytechnic diploma (or equivalent) in field related to the degree course. In 1992, the Singapore Ministry of Education invited SIM to run the Open University degree program in Singapore, with an initial grant from the Singapore Government. This program is linked to the UK Open University . A number of BA and BSc degrees are offered. Entry to these courses generally requires academic achievement of at least two GCE A level subject passes, a SIM or polytechnic diploma, or equivalent. The courses offered under the Open University program adopt a flexible learning approach, so that students can organize study around employment and other activities. Nevertheless, there is strong support provided for students, including regular tutorials. Degrees under this program are awarded by the UK Open University.

LaSalle SIA College of the Arts has arrangements with Queensland University of Technology and RMIT University in Australia to deliver certain degree courses. Entry to these programs is based on completion of LaSalle diplomas. For example, LaSalle has collaborated with Queensland University of Technology to offer a Bachelor of Arts in Drama. Similarly, the RMIT University Bachelor in Fine Arts course is offered through LaSalle, with advanced standing into the RMIT course based on completion of the LaSalle Diploma of Fine Arts. In addition to articulation arrangements already cited, there are a many other instances of degree level programs, including distance education programs, being provided by international universities in association with professional bodies and other entities. There is also considerable traffic from Singaporean polytechnic diploma graduates undertaking degree level studies abroad, frequently with significant advanced standing. Extensive articulation possibilities exist in Singapore, for technical and vocational education students. These arrangements have been described as 'a multi level matrix of programs that provides linkages between the school system postsecondary technical and vocational education and training and polytechnic education through a system of bridges and ladders'.

Thailand

Currently, about 80% of the Thai population of 60 million odd people reside in rural areas with about .20 million employed in agriculture. Around 15 million of the population are engaged in other sectors of the economy including manufacturing, construction, banking and insurance, and service industries such as tourism. Although agriculture provides employment for the bulk of the Thai workforce it only accounts for 11% of Gross Domestic Product. The ability of Thailand to respond to economic opportunities is restricted by the educational level of the Thai labour force which is currently weighted towards a workforce that has only undertaken primary level studies.

Primary education is compulsory, but not all children, especially in rural areas, complete 6 years of education. Nevertheless, there is an Government objective for all students to complete 9 years of education, with the longer term anticipation that within the next decade 12 years of education will be universally available to all Thai children. Currently, six years of primary education may be followed by 3 years of lower secondary education and 3 years of upper secondary education, with post secondary education provided by universities and vocational institutes. Upper secondary level education is divided into two streams - general education and vocational education. Successful completion of the general stream results in the award of the Matayom 6 (Certificate of Secondary Education). Completion of the vocational stream results in the award of a Por Wor Chor (Certificate of Vocational Education) after 3 years of study.

The intent of the Certificate of Vocational Education was that students would leave school and enter the world of work. In practice this is not the case as between 70 and 90% of students who complete this program proceeding to a postsecondary vocational institute for higher level studies. In one sense this must be considered to constitute a very high level of articulation for students who complete a TVE program, although the main intent of the Certificate of Vocational Education is to prepare students for employment. The low percentage of Certificate of Vocational Education graduates entering the workforce is a reflection of the desirability of gaining entry to diploma and degree granting institutions, where the ultimate rewards are significantly greater.

Postsecondary technical and vocational education

At the postsecondary level, a number of Thai institutions

offer a 2 year post year 12 Por Wor Sor (Diplomas of Vocational Education) directed at preparing technician level graduates. These institutions include:

— Department of Vocational Education (DOVE) technical institutes.

— Rajamangala Institute of Technology.

— King Mongkut's Institute of Technology

— Private vocational colleges

Fields of study include engineering, business studies, fine arts, agriculture, textiles, and home economics and tourism. In addition, the Ministry of Public Health provides programs for nurses, and the Ministry of Defence provides a range of postsecondary programs in military academies.

It should also be noted that some Thai universities and institutes offer 2 year programs at subdegree level such as diplomas or associate degrees. Some universities also award an associate degree to students who complete the first three years of study towards a bachelor degree. An important factor in the provision of formal postsecondary education in Thailand is the role of private universities and vocational colleges. The numbers of students attending private postsecondary educational institutions is about the same as those attending government institutions. Thailand has a history of private postsecondary institutions dating back to the late 1960s, and it has been the policy of successive Thai governments to encourage growth in the private provision of post secondary sector, given that government financial resources to support the delivery educational programs is limited.

A form of quality control is exerted on private universities and vocational colleges through an approvals process which requires that minimum curriculum and resource requirements be satisfied. Nevertheless, places at government universities and vocational institutes and colleges are highly sought after. This is particularly the case in terms of prestigious Bangkok institutions.

Non-formal vocational education

A significant thrust to provide skills training exists in Thailand through the delivery of so called non-formal education programs. Non-formal education programs are provided by many government departments, state enterprizes, private and non-government organizations, and private schools. The most important providers being the Department of Vocational Education (DOVE), the Department of Non-formal Education (DNFE), and the Ministry of Labour and Social Welfare through the Department of Skill Department (DSD).

Many non-formal education courses are directed at the development of basic vocational skills, in pre-employment programs, ranging from 3 months to one year in length. The target group is students who have completed primary education, but for one reason or another are not able to proceed to secondary education. Typically such students would come from families with limited means. The pre-employment courses include training in electrical, automotive and construction technology and would an industry training component. Large numbers of students in the non-formal education sector undertake upgrading short courses. For example DSD offers courses in supervision, programmable logic control, welding inspection, and chemical hazard safety.

The importance of non-formal education in Thailand is such that in 1995 DOVE had about 265,000 non-formal enrolments, and DSD had 110,000 enrolments in non-formal programs, which are further supplemented by the efforts of private training providers and industry based training. The enrolment in non-formal education institutions is indicative of meeting real need. Currently these programs are not linked to higher levels of the Thai education system to any extent. As a long term objective non-formal programs would be enhanced if effective linkages could be introduced.

Due to the highly competitive demand for places, virtually all students entering government universities do so after completion of the academic stream at a secondary school. This means that students who diverge from the secondary academic stream at the end of year 9, in reality may only proceed to postsecondary vocational programs if they are to do so in a government funded institution, such as Rajamangala Institute of Technology. To enter a private university it would be necessary, not only to satisfy academic entry requirements, which might include an entry examination, but also pay course fees. Provision for Diploma of Vocational Education graduates to undertake degrees, is made by King Mongkut's Institute of Technology (KMIT) and Rajamangala Institute of Technology.

KMIT North Bangkok offers Bachelor of Technology and Bachelor of Science in Technical Education to Diploma of Vocational Education graduates. It is also possible for graduates from these programs to eventually articulate to Masters and Doctor of Technical Education courses conducted by KMIT. Rajamangala Institute of Technology is a very significant provider of degree level programs for Diploma of Vocational Education graduates, offering undergraduate degrees in a number of fields including agriculture, engineering, business, arts, architecture and science. About 24% of the student body is engaged in degree level courses at Rajamangala.

The DOVE Pathumwan Technical College (Bangkok) also offers a Bachelor of Engineering (Mechatronics Engineering). This college also has an affiliation with King Mongkut's Institute of Technology North Bangkok which has permitted the establishment of a Bachelor of Industrial Technology (Industrial Instrumentation Technology) course. In total about 13,000 students are undertaking degree and higher level courses at King Mongkut's Institute of Technology, Rajamangala Institute of Technology and Pathumwan Technical College.

The incentive for 2 year vocational education diploma students to continue on and complete a degree is great. Not only in terms of status in gaining a degree, but also the prospect of much higher salaries which is a strong motivating force. Degree holders can expect better career paths, particularly in government employment, which has not provided significant recognition of vocational education awards to motivate diploma students to seek a career based on their vocational education qualification. Diplomates expect less rewarding positions, where the salary payable would be significantly lower than that commanded by degree holders. Some universities such as Majeo Institute of Agricultural Technology, Prince of Songkla and Srinakharinwirot University will allow holders of the Diploma of Vocational Education to enter the third year of certain degree courses, subject to an entry examination.

Nevertheless, the linkages between Thai vocational education colleges and universities might generally be seen as not being strong, and any diagram of the Thai education system invariably has no linkages shown between vocational education colleges and university programs. Another articulation option for postsecondary education courses provided by the two open universities, Ramkhamhaeng University and Sukhothai Thammathirat Open University. These universities had a combined 1995 enrolment of 523,583 students. Entry to the open universities does not require an entry examination, fees are low, and a wide range of courses are available. In spite of the large enrolment by the open universities, the self directed nature of study and length of time required to complete programs, and perhaps the open entry levels, has resulted in low course completion rates. International linkages between Thai universities and vocational institutes is another factor which might also be touched upon. Such linkages are encouraged by the Thai government, particularly in facilitating the development and delivery in Thailand of post-graduate degrees, jointly with international universities. A number of examples also exist where Thai universities have twinning arrangements, such that part of a degree is undertaken in Thailand and completed offshore at the partner university.

This pattern is replicated in a number of vocational education institutions. The Graduate School of Rajamangala Institute of Technology has an arrangement with the UK University of Northumbria in respect of a Master of Science (Telecommunications Engineering). King Mongkut's Institute of Technology North Bangkok has an arrangement with the UK University of Strathclyde to jointly deliver a Master of Engineering course. The Bachelor of Engineering (Mechatronics Engineering) delivered by the DOVE Pathumwan Technical College has come about due to support by the Japanese International Cooperation Agency (JICA) since 1991. JICA has not only provided teaching equipment but also supplied the services of academic experts to assist in program delivery.

Clearly, the Thai system of education is responding to economic and social changes. Future directions include making secondary education more generally available, whilst improving standards and quality of course delivery, for all levels of education. The pressure of numbers on Thai government funded technical and vocational institutions is very great, and simply increasing enrolments without a commensurate increase in resources, is recognised as having a direct impact on program quality. Given limits on the ability of government to fund education, the involvement of the private sector in the provision postsecondary education will grow in importance.

Vocational education in Thailand already has a high degree of articulation in current programs, but this is mainly confined to provision for articulation within the vocational education sector. There is limited opportunity for vocational education students to transfer to the higher education sector, particularly to government universities, where entry is effectively restricted to the top group of graduates from the upper secondary academic stream. Given resource limitations this is a difficult issue to address. Currently there is very limited ability for students to advance in an educational sense from (non-formal) skills based programs, and it would be desirable to integrate courses of this type into the broader Thai system of education. As Thai vocational education institutions move to respond to economic change, the challenge to meet the necessity to provide pathways for continuing education in a formal course format and by less structured means, will increase.

4

Vocational Education and Training in 21st Century

The new 'information or knowledge society', information processes as well as technology in the field of production are rapidly changing. The value of an enterprise is estimated from its capability to acquire, to produce, to disseminate, and to apply knowledge commercially within the productive process. Mass production is replaced by new production processes, which promote more flexible adaptation to consumers' demands. In the new international world order, multinational enterprises which are active in the global market place are restructuring production in all industrial fields and services.

Even the most traditional sectors of the economy, such as the textile industry, construction, tourism, or medical care are being affected. In this new information society, competition and conflict are no longer competition and conflict between states for new territories or for enlarged markets. Instead, with the possible exception of raw material and energy resources, competition centres on the establishment of competitive conditions in the production and dissemination of knowledge and on the use of information networks, telecommunication satellites, or the mass media, for ensuring access to potential consumers.

The impact of these developments and the adaptation that they require have not yet been understood fully. They affect directly not only individual choices but also the exercise of policies. At the production level, experiencing a crisis in the traditional, technologically obsolete industrial units such as the steel, metallurgical, shipbuilding, and automobile industries. Yet these were the industries which supported economic growth during the previous decades. Nowadays, all enterprises, regardless of size, are called upon to adapt themselves in view of the emergence of new, dynamic, information-intensive business units. In all sectors of economic activity, especially in services, production based on modern technology is being fragmented and is supported by a series of new services and networks. Hierarchical organizational structures give way to more collective and flexible modes of administration.

Highly-skilled labour assumes special importance and receives high wages. The employer or manager who bases the profitability of his unit on the high productivity of his staff is now becoming—and this is important — personally interested in the education, training, safety, mental and corporal hygiene of his workers, as well as their positive disposition to work. Thus, in rapidly developing societies, the productive network is extended further to cover workers' support services including training, security, social protection, and family assistance. In this way, social services are provided within the market place while, for many years, these had remained unsatisfactory or covered exclusively through social policy. In the new international economic order, the development and extension of the productive and creative capabilities of society presuppose the ability of its members to adapt easily, to obtain continuous training and further education, and to create effective networks of social support. Whenever productive restructuring is not undertaken in an organized, fast and effective manner, or is not underpinned by the simultaneous development of basic education, of training, of continuous education and of effective networks of social support, societies are being hit by unemployment and social exclusion. Societies then run the risk of becoming divided into 'insiders' and 'outsiders' even if productivity is enhanced and high growth rates are being achieved.

The rapid changes in production and organisation have led to a rapid degradation of the acquired knowledge and to major upheavals in the labour market. It is estimated that 80% of the stock of knowledge of an individual becomes obsolete within a decade, and that a university graduate is forced to change his profession up to seven times throughout his lifetime. New professions continuously emerge while traditional ones disappear. Under these circumstances, there not only exist mounting pressures for new investment in education and training, but major changes in the character of the educational process have taken place. Young people, overwhelmed by new information, are gaining access to new sources of knowledge through electronic networks and contemporary communication media. They have to learn how to identify useful information, and how to infer their own conclusions from it. In order to do so, they must have developed earlier their analytical and critical thinking as well as most basic skills. They must have learned to think abstractly and creatively, to formulate their thoughts clearly both in oral and written form, and they must have developed integrative skills. They must have learned how to learn effectively. If they have done so, they will be aware that knowledge is a continuous process, which does not start at a certain point in life and does not end with a degree.

In view of these major challenges, the structure of demand for education and training services has greatly changed. At the same time, witnessing changes in the supply of these services. Thus the educational system is called upon to create new structures, to extend its services, and to use new educational methods in order to rise to the task. Let us have a closer look at these changes starting from the demand side for training services. Because of the changes which are taking place in production, frictional as well as structural unemployment is rapidly increasing. The time one spends between two jobs is prolonged, since there is no sufficient information on the labour market itself, and there is increased uncertainty about the characteristics or prospects of any open position. If the time devoted to job search is long, the skills that a prospective candidate possesses tend to become obsolete and his/her chance of finding a satisfactory job is reduced. Therefore, finding a satisfactory job presupposes, more often than not, training or retraining.

Under these circumstances, every potential employee, especially one that has been unemployed for a long time, feels the pressure to retrain and retool. He or she does not know in advance, however, which training programme may extend his/her skills more effectively, or which one may best respond to the needs of the labour market. The greater the need one has for retraining, the more inexperienced one is, the older one gets, and the more traumatic one's previous work experience has been, the more incapable he or she appears in making the right choices. Under the fear of long-term unemployment or marginalisation, young people, in particular, approach education or training services with apprehension. They feel the pressure from their social and family environment to do something, and they have the illusion that training would resolve the problem of their integration into the labour market. They make choices based on the advice of friends or family members who give them information on the current demand for graduates from a specific programme.

The sad thing is that, many times, this information is not useful, since conditions in the labour market change rapidly and new skills are being demanded. Therefore, whereas the demand for educational, training and retraining services grows fast, the capabilities for an effective use of these services are reduced or, at least, not correspondingly broadened. In addition, in the presence of more flexible labour markets, workers do not necessarily have adequate incentives to receive training. The more flexible the labour market becomes, and the lower real wages get, the greater is the cost that workers or the unemployed have to bear to acquire training or retraining. As with any investment decision, investment in human capital has to be amortized. Enhanced flexibility in the labour market might in fact imply reduced incentives for investment in human capital, which is a necessary condition for productivity growth. On the supply side, there is evidence of rapid growth in educational and training services provided by both the public and private sectors. The expansion of services, however, has, in many instances, remained anarchic and ineffective.

— There still exists considerable confusion as to the distinction that should be drawn between basic educational as opposed to training services. This has been exacerbated by the fact that formal educational systems have often been driven to provide professional training services, while vocational institutes have often offered courses in basic sciences. It is slowly becoming evident that general education and basic skills ought to be provided by formal educational systems, whereas training systems ought to concentrate on the development of additional professional skills that are needed by the market.

— The priorities of publicly-funded educational and training programmes ought to be distinguished from those of the private sector. There is a growing consensus that the chief priority for the public sector is the provision of high-quality general education. Instead, in many developing countries, the public sector still provides professional training from the secondary-school level upwards at high cost and with limited effectiveness. Priority on the provision of high-quality, basic education is becoming even more important in the information society of the 1990s. When citizens are functionally illiterate, when they have not developed their analytical thinking, when they cannot speak at least one foreign language, and cannot retrieve information with the use of computers, then they are seriously handicapped in a rapidly changing labour market.

— Relation to the development of training services is the breadth, scope and content of competencies and fields offered. These are usually developed with an eye towards past or present development needs, even though, training ought to enhance capabilities for future needs. The absence of adequate information about future needs constitutes a major market imperfection that hampers the smooth functioning of both the training and labour markets.

— Quality is a major issue in the design of training programmes and in their implementation. As the market for providing educational and training services faces new challenges, national. governments and international organisations and agencies are called upon to make significant decisions and to spend considerable amounts of money under conditions of uncertainty. At the level of principles, set forth three main principles or objectives:

a) Safeguarding the right of access to educational and training services: unobstructed access to the educational and training systems has to be considered an undeniable social right, especially in the context of the information society. At all levels, education and training systems have to remain open to those who want to obtain services regardless of economic ability, age, or prior job experience.

This principle dictates specific policy priorities, such as creating schools for those who have not completed basic education or are dropouts, helping school and university students with special assistance courses, doing away with arbitrary quotas on the provision of tertiary education, and introducing flexible, educational training and retraining programmes at all levels. It should also be remembered that the social right to educational access goes hand in hand with two other social rights: the social right to employment, and the social right to information. Thus, active educational policies go hand in hand with active employment policies and policies to promote the dissemination of information available to citizens.

b) The second principle to which agree is the need to extend the availability of educational options, and to enhance the educational choices of European citizens. The fast changes in technology and the burst of information make this a pressing need. Citizens should be able to choose the place, the time and the breadth of their education and training in order to cover their diverse professional, economic and social needs.

Since, from the level of maturity, the experiences and choices differ from person to person, the fulfilment of this second principle presupposes the development of basic skills—language, analytical abilities, expression —at the level of obligatory education, the expansion of these skills at the secondary level, and the substantial consolidation of knowledge at the level of tertiary education. Additionally, it requires the availability of adequate training and retraining services throughout one's professional life. Social security and health benefits should be extended during training periods. Furthermore active consultation and orientation services should be developed so that citizens can make rational and cost-effective choices regarding their educational and professional future.

c) The third principle concerns the relationship between education and training on the one hand,

> and the workings of the labour market on the other. Educational and training systems should be open fora for the provision of skills and knowledge. They cannot and should not function as mechanisms which put up barriers to entry in the labour market, nor do they guarantee 'professional rights' to their graduates. It is through the acquisition of highquality skills and abilities that graduates enhance their chances to be integrated in the labour market and to perform successfully in it.

The first issue that arises concerns the definition of an 'optimal regulatory area' for educational and training policy. In the global market place, should education or training be designed at the supranational, the national or the very local level? The 'subsidiarity principle', according to which policies should be designed at the most functionally appropriate level, is not very helpful. Even though there appears to be a trend toward the localisation of educational and training services, my feeling is that the exigencies of a global market place will push us all towards greater homogeneity and more global networking in the provision of these services.

The second issue touches upon the role of the public sector. It is generally accepted that public intervention in the market place is justified on grounds of mitigating existing inequalities or of amplifying market inefficiencies. In this case, the public sector has an important role to play in safeguarding access to the educational and training systems, in the development of necessary skills for future market needs, or in complementing the private market in areas where fixed costs prohibit the development of profitable services by the private sector. Such a role for the public sector, however, presupposes social funding through the tax system. Consequently, the necessary steps must be taken to finance adequately public training services either from national budgets or from the European Union's structural funds.

The introduction of total quality management in the provision of educational and training services. The design and implementation of effective quality control systems in this field are still at an elementary stage. In this direction, specialized information systems need to be elaborated and integrated, and quality indicators developed. These can provide a basis for an objective evaluation of these services by both users and policymakers. Finally, special attention should be given to the development of contemporary services for counselling and professional orientation regarding training and educational choices.

The most young people do not possess adequate information based on which to make educational or professional choices. At the same time, training centres need to become more closely connected with the business world through appropriate networking and/or apprenticeships, so that new skill requirements can be easily detected and obsolete ones eliminated. Networking between educational and training centres and business can also facilitate the placement of graduates and reduce considerably the costs of job hunting. The challenge for European policy, therefore, is, on the one hand, to develop a modern educational and training system and, at the same time, to develop the adaptational capabilities required to service changing market needs.

New Technologies and the Production Process

One should avoid the snag of technological 'determinism' that would link in a simplistic way the introduction of new technologies, new qualifications and innovations in Vocational Training. One should refrain from saying that new technologies determine in a direct univocal way new qualifications which in turn generate new needs for training. The role of new forms of work organization is a determining factor in the emergence of new qualification.

The new forms of work organization The main features are as follows:

— promoting flexible adaptable work structures and organization,

— decentralizing and delegating powers of decision,

— desegregating functions: production, marketing, research, maintenance,

— decreasing the number of hierarchy levels, development of team work: one no longer defines a job, but rather the production objectives of a team. Increased dialogue, mobilization of executors' intelligence, pursuit of ideas and suggestions from the base.

With the exception of computer technology, there are few entirely new professions or jobs, but the transformation of existing work situations is generalized.

Increased multifunctionality of executive personnel: in industry, executive personnel must intervene on the first level of maintenance, less specialization for each type of machinery. The separation between mechanics, electricity, electronics is unsuitable. In the 70s'-80s, there was a great controversy in order to know whether new technologies were going to 'dequalify' jobs or—on the contrary—they were going to lead to an 'enrichment' of tasks. In the field of services, secretarial work organized in a 'pool' represented an extreme form of rationalisation and dequalification. In modern enterprises and administrations, secretaries execute text processing for printing and have varied assistance tasks.

— Difficulties for the intermediary level of the hierarchy: the middle level management faces a crisis unless technically qualified;

— At the intermediary level, many jobs require rational competencies, particularly so in services: being able to listen to the client or user, carry out a diagnostic;

— At a higher level, many jobs require a higher specialization in view of the increased technical nature in certain fields: in finance for instance (actuaries), in commerce (logistics) and, of course, computer scientists;

— The 'communication' and 'human resources' functions, oriented towards animation, training and coordination are indispensable in a decentralized organization.

The needs in terms of knowledge, know-how and behaviour raised by the labour market are in rapid development. New trends are as follows:

— traditional technical know-how loses importance;

— the general level of knowledge which must be more systematic and more indepth, as equipment and organizations are more complex and clients more demanding;

- in industry, automation demands a desegregation of technical specialities as it touches upon many disciplines:
- multidisciplinarity becomes an asset;
- there is a double-competency bonus in many sectors: technical-commercial, legal-linguistic, biologist-computer scientist, etc;
- behaviour acquires a fundamental importance: people's potential, personalities, adaptability, initiative, creativity. In the service sector (50% of jobs) priority is placed on basic knowledge and behaviour: relations with the client.

Implications for technical and vocational education and training

Access: everybody must leave the training system with a minimum diploma as unskilled jobs are disappearing; if this were not the case, then would be creating 'excluded people'.

Strengthen the progression itinerary: raising the level of competencies must be translated into opportunities for progress (in the scale of diplomas) within the system of technical and vocational education and training: vocational training should no longer be a 'dead-end'. Access routes towards higher education cycles and reintegration in general education should be multiplied.

Training programmes should be despecialized by grouping channels, specialities and diplomas, and by stressing competencies 'transferable' from one sector to the other. In all European countries, one sees a decrease in the number of training courses and diplomas by the grouping of specialities and diplomas. Modernisation of contents must be a constant concern. Its implementation requires efficient institutional mechanisms of dialogue between social partners and public trainers.

It is necessary to promote training in alternation and apprenticeship so as to allow for the acquisition of real-life behaviour. In-house training offers the opportunity to become familiar not only with new equipment, but also with corporate culture.

Start an on-going process for the renewal of diplomas and programmes through bipartite or tripartite committees.

Continuing training

Continuing vocational training acquires a central role. It must 'listen to' the needs of enterprises and become a component of personnel policies. Enterprises will be brought to invest in personnel training more than in the past. It is important that the development of 'human resources' within enterprises becomes a factor of competitiveness and that continuing training policies are integrated in personnel policies.

New technologies and the production process

In the last few years seen an intensification of the globalization of the economy. Certain of its chief characteristics are, among others, the following:

— the rapid increase in the transparency of the demand and the supply of products and services beyond national borders,

- the globalization in terms of the convergence of major functional-quality models and other expectations on the part of the consumers,
- emphasis on improved quality and reduced delivery times as well as strict observance of deadlines,
- more intense differentiation, even individualization, of customers' wishes, and
- the geographic-/functional distribution of production to more than one country aiming at its total improvement.

All this, in tandem with macro-economic circumstances that require an increase of the productive force beyond demand and the reduction of the product life-cycle, has intensified international competition. Businesses have added to and exploited these new technologies so as to face this challenge and become competent:

- in the development and timely introduction of new technologies in both production and the products, 'innovation and time to markets',
- to response to dynamic business changes in the environment, especially under conditions of uncertainty,
- the globalization of business strategies.

Informatics, especially, and electronic mass media have created fully new circumstances (or at least the preconditions) for direct and effective communication and collaboration between three main areas:

- research, development and design planning,
- production, and

— management and administration through networking.

These attempts to reorganise the productive process means that partly gone beyond the models in some sectors at least. Initially, the efforts were focused on the technical restructuring of the production chain itself. The reduction of 'production depth' with the relocation of some tasks outside the company, 'the just in time production' and the provision of modern technological equipment (CAD, CAM, CIM etc.) have led to some examples of 'factories without workers', as well as to lean production which, in the change from the 80s to the 90s was felt to be the panacea that would resolve all the relevant problems.

Very soon it became apparent that technological renewal and production restructuring would not suffice on their own to reinforce the competitiveness of a company by ensuring the much-desired flexibility and accuracy of the necessary reactions to the rapidly changing demands of the market. These efforts should be enforced with the introduction of new models of employment and personnel management that would have to have suitable skills for each case. Such a strategy would require a constant enrichment of professional skills and an amelioration of their level. But even though technical changes can be identified with a relatively high degree of certainty, the manner in which they affect the organization of work and the corresponding professional competence has not been sufficiently investigated, especially since the correlations are not one to one.

There is a general trend to facilitate workers in their continuous training by widening their horizons to similar and neighbouring activities. The existence and the flexible exploitation of different means or opportunities for vocational education, training, additional training and career furthering through various combinations and choices remains always one of the critical desiderata. It is internationally recognized that in the field of total reformation of production, part of the triptych of technical aspects, organization and vocational competence, there are still many opportunities that remain unexploited.

Therefore, on this basis, it emerges that nowadays training, education and further training for human resources that would ensure the constant improvement of their quality would serve as an active factor for structural changes with an improvement in business competitiveness, and in European competitiveness in general, in the economic world market. What gains critical importance is the systemic combination of initial with continuous education and training so as to open up the following prospects:

— Response to new models of employment and professions

— Through specialization in the narrow professional field,

— With the acquisition of abilities for further activities, and by career furthering.

— Combination of these additional elements in professional profiles so that they can correspond to various professional activities, economic sectors or professional guilds in a flexible manner.

— Elementary transparency for businesses so that the real practical value of the additional abilities that workers who work in them have can be recognized.

— Credible information provided to youth as to the existing alternatives of career prospects and professional advancement.

— Orientation and support of adults in view of change in the field of their work or their employment.

— Creation of models by agencies of education and training about market demand and the quality of their services.

Workers who will correspond to such more demanding jobs will have to have the following skills:

— Manual skills

— Mental abilities

— Analytical and synthetic thinking

— Computing and foreign languages

— Guidance skills

— Initiative

— Emergency decisionmaking

— Supervisory activities

— Communicative skills and conflict management

— Good teamwork.

All these require a wider and high level initial general education so that inducted youths may acquire, among other things, the ability of 'learning by themselves'. This wide infrastructure of knowledge will facilitate adaptation to changing work market demands by the addition of the most suitable new knowledge. In respect of the levels and the content of the professions, a specific trend is starting to show, whereby the goods of these innovations throughout the spectrum of production chiefly benefit people with higher level qualifications; the upgraded jobs in terms of quality set increased demands of the workers. That is where unique opportunities are to be found for the creation of new jobs. This brings about the obsolescence of medium-level skills, especially if acquired through educational training programmes. That happens because trainees just learn how to carry out a specific task. However they have not been trained to organize their work themselves or to adapt to major changes in their working environment. So that would imply that there is a need for the enrichment of vocational education and training by general education elements which are considerably different from the traditional meaning of the term.

The role of the workplace as a learning environment, and especially of additional training of a new kind that goes beyond traditional 'learning by doing', since it would incorporate and assimilate systematically technological innovations in production as a learning inflow, will be very important, even determining. It concerns specific jobs, usually of a short duration, but continuous as a process as well. Being a decentralized form of learning, it uses multimedia to the widest possible extent and, with the continuous revision of the subject to be learned, it also assesses the furthest possible practical convertibility of the acquired competencies and skills. However, innovations are not of their own a motive or a tool for learning throughout work.

The predominant means of informatics in this case should be formed in such a way that, apart from the accomplishment of the task itself, they should also have 'didactic', if not individualised, competencies. It is only then that the worker will be encouraged and become capable not only of understanding and of applying passively, but of forming actively the new possibilities afforded each time. There are many indications whereby technical expertise and technology, because of the globalisation both of knowledge and of the markets, will converge and will almost be equated on a common point with relatively few differences. This will result in competition being transposed to workers' levels, and especially to their capabilities, the quality and combination of which, through suitable forms of work organization, will be decisive for the fate of a company within the business arena.

The role of vocational education and training seems to acquire ever-greater importance. The challenges are major and various and the problems are complex and urgent. But the prospects and solutions at hand appear very alluring and original.

New Technologies—Vocational Education and Training

The impact of information and communication technologies (ICT) on competencies and qualifications; i.e. identify in different occupations and professions how competencies are affected by ICT, what are the new competencies required by the workers in the information society, how this modifies the recruitment policies of the enterprises; that is, at which qualification level enterprises recruit their staff, how professions and occupations evolve, and what is the response of the Vocational Education and Training (VET) systems; that is, how the VET systems react to the changes caused by ICT.

The results are mainly addressed to policy makers, in the form of recommendations, which they can take into account when formulating their VET policies. Over the past 20 years witnessed important technological changes mainly caused by the rapid development and extensive use of information and communication technologies. This trend is modifying work, the structure of qualifications and work organizations within enterprises, and provoking substantial changes in the labour market and in society as a whole.

Technological development and consequent organizational changes Enterprises have to deal with an increase in competition due to the increasing internationalization and deregulation of the markets. Enterprises have therefore to fight hard and to be very creative to preserve or improve the competitive edge that they need in order to keep existing customers and attract new ones. ICTs have their biggest impact in the workplace. New functions are emerging. Work organization is changing: enterprises are increasingly abandoning the traditional models and they are simplifying their hierarchical structure, delegating responsibilities at all levels and ensuring the participation of all their employees in the innovation process.

The introduction of IT in enterprises and organizations tends to run parallel with organizational changes fundamentally involving the transition from highly hierarchical structures to programme groups (groupware). The use of networks is also becoming more and more important (intranet, internet). The direct consequence of these organisational changes is the fact that workers are asked to develop new competencies.

The introduction of IT in the various functional areas tends to make mechanical, lesser-skilled tasks superfluous. The new competencies required in the wake of the introduction of IT are fundamentally related to the ability to obtain, select, process and disseminate information. Also, new methodological competencies related to the knowledge of the organization in question and how to move within this organization are necessary. In sectors in which IT exerts a strong influence, social and organizational competencies are priorities. The integral development of the human personality, the fundamental objective of all education and training, is therefore the very basis of the new competencies. This means that abilities such as self-esteem, creativity, adaptability, responsibility, self-control or the ability to work in a team or communication capability, openmindedness, tolerance, adaptability to changes, self-identification (of all employees) with the enterprise objectives, and problemsolving capability are becoming the essential personality attributes of the competent professional. In a technological environment characterized by constant innovation, permanent ability to learn has become a fundamental competence for the majority of professionals.

Knowledge and information, the essential raw material for production in the information society, are to be found in the context of the overall organization, rather then at the level of individual professionals. This increases the responsibility of the enterprise as a learning organization. This causes changes in the content of various professions:

— Individuals need more knowledge and an increasing number of skills and competencies to accomplish tasks which are becoming more and more complex.

Although technical competencies remain very important in the Information Society, the main focus is on personal, relational and organizational competencies.

Serious integration problems are emerging for certain groups, with the gradual exclusion from employment in the area of ICT of those with a certification level below the upper-secondary school-leaving certificate or middle-level vocational training.

In the future, internal promotion is therefore likely to be much more random than in the past; advancement based on length of service is now obsolete, for two reasons are given below:

— What matters nowadays, in all the cases examined, is the ability to react and adapt to a precise situation and to work efficiently;

— Banks are tending to recruit—with one exception in the United Kingdom—at a higher level of qualification.

Answer of the VET systems to the identified changes in terms of training supply; which training initiatives are developed in response to new professional needs Initial training provision, both at university and vocational training level, is going through a significant period of renewal in terms of technological content. In the case of universities, short-cycle diplomas with very distinct vocational learning are gaining in importance. There has been a significant increase in the number of initial certificates and training places over the last decade, including a surplus of certificate-holders in some areas.

The introduction of the new technologies and subsequent changes in jobs have to be underpinned by a sound policy of training in enterprise. The methods used in each country and in each of the enterprises interviewed to fill skill gaps or improve skills are nevertheless closely linked to their respective strategy choices.

As a general rule training schemes are: integrated into the occupation in question and offered to everyone working in that occupation; organized to upgrade skills; organized during the introduction of devices using the new technologies that offer, for instance, savings in time and increased operational reliability; organized to make people aware of and train them in the use of tools enabling ready access to information that could improve the quality of the service given. At present, there does not seem to be a standard route for training in the new technologies. One-off schemes tend to be organized depending on needs.

The management of the banks interviewed would like to attach more importance to continuing training and in particular to encourage employees to continue to progress by taking part in training schemes or self-training, especially by attending training leading to certificates or diplomas. Some countries have, moreover, started to reform initial training in this sector by rebuilding training routes and enabling diplomas to be obtained by credit units.

This desire to raise employees' awareness and to encourage them to continue to learn helps employees' achieve the state of mind that they will need to successfully keep up with the changes that will take place in the banking industry throughout the world over the next ten years. In general terms, continuing training provision is not adequately planned by the enterprises in accordance with the new requirements in occupational areas in which IT exerts a strong influence; in the majority of cases, continuing training is left to the initiative of the employee in the form of self-directed learning. It is important to point out, though, that many enterprises, overall of medium and large size, organise training initiatives within the enterprise itself, privileging different 'training areas' which may help the workers to acquire the competencies and abilities which are required by the information society.

The impact of information and communication technologies on vocational competencies and training in the telecommunication sector and administration/ offices showed that enterprises are offering and organizing training and courses for their employees which aim at developing social and relational competencies, or courses based on a detailed knowledge of the enterprise and its organization, so as to stimulate an entrepreneurial culture. Very interesting also are the training methodologies used for providing training. Action learning initiatives are based on working groups composed of the workers in the enterprise where the learning process is activated starting from a specific and real working situation. Workers are faced with a real situation which exists in their working environment in the enterprise in which they work and they are asked to analyze the situation, identify the different problematic it presents and to propose possible solutions to be applied.

The best solution found will be used for solving the problem. It is a sort of learning by doing. What workers learn is immediately applied in the working environment. As far as continuing training is concerned, there are some interesting initiatives which are being organized by enterprises to upgrade the competencies of their workers. Recommendations for the improvement of training. First of all, it is of the utmost importance that policy makers take into account the acquisition of the key competencies required by IS in their training objectives. Then, when providing training, it is important to make use of the technologies which will have to be used by the workers in their working environment so that they can get used to ICT. Finally, it is important to articulate the training supply in a perspective of continuing training which has to be compatible with the employed or unemployed status of the beneficiaries.

The new role of training is focused on its capacity to identify new professional needs expressed in the production context and to translate them into new educational and training contents through a continuous exchange between the production system and the training system where each system can learn from the other. This should lead to a change in the culture of learning at all ages. It would no longer be about absorbing information and not even just about reading, writing and arithmetic.

5

Guidance Counsellor

The Institute of Guidance Counsellors (IGC) represents members who work in a range of educational, community and local employment settings. This role document, developed by members of the adult guidance subcommittee of the IGC, is intended to provide a model for those guidance counsellors who work solely or mainly with adults. This chapter seeks to reflect best guidance and counselling practice for an evolving Irish adult educational and vocational guidance service that is currently being developed and expanded throughout the country. Its primary purpose is to provide guidelines to assist IGC adult guidance counsellors in planning and fulfilling their role in the varying educational and vocational environments in which they are employed. It also intends to provide practical structures as well as a source of inspiration and information, which will enhance the adult guidance and counselling service.

Guidance counsellors now work in many different institutions with clients from a wide range of age groups and backgrounds. There is a need therefore to have guidelines that reflect their work practices and conditions. Training is accessed through a wide range of professional courses. These will develop and expand in line with the changing world of work and education.

The adult guidance counsellor is professionally trained to provide for the personal, educational and vocational development of adults. The work of the adult guidance counsellor takes place in a variety of locations and settings such as:

— Adult education centres

— Area Based Partnership Companies

— Colleges of Further Education

— Community Based Services

— Drug Rehabilitation Services

— Ex-Offender Services

— FAS

— Higher Education Institutions

— Local Employment Service Network

— Prison Education Services

— Private practice

— Schools

— Statutory agencies

Functions that make up an adult guidance and counselling service

— Assessment service

— Career and vocational guidance and counselling (including career-path planning and employment placement)

— Developmental programmes

— Educational guidance and counselling

— Information and communications technology

— Information gathering and dissemination

— Personal guidance and counseling

— Referral services

Educational Guidance & Counselling

Educational guidance and counselling involves the provision of information on educational opportunities, the guidance of clients in decision-making and the support of clients in their choice of individual education goals.

The guidance counsellor discusses with the client the client's educational potential, educational opportunities, subject choice, course choice and outcomes. Educational guidance involves the provision of information on further education and financial assistance. The guidance counsellor seeks, at all times, to match the individual's ability with education opportunities. Educational Guidance can involve working with the client in the following areas:

— Counselling for learning-related problems

— Decision-making skills

— Exam techniques

— Goal-setting skills

— Motivational skills

— Study skills

— Testing

Career & Vocational Guidance and Counselling

Career and vocational guidance and counselling involves facilitating the client's career and vocational decision-making in a non-directive way. Adults seeking careers information are engaged in a proactive process.

Careers education is a process whereby the guidance counsellor makes information on specific jobs and career areas available to the client. This is followed by an evaluation of the client's ability to understand and use this information to make career decisions. The guidance counsellor encourages the client to discuss preferred options through the medium of group information sessions or one-to-one sessions and to make decisions accordingly. In order to facilitate this discussion, information can be accessed by the client through psychometric testing, researching careers literature, using information and communications technology and visiting exhibitions. For many guidance counsellors, their work in career and vocational guidance and counselling can be categorized as follows:

Individualized career-path planning

Individualized career-path planning involves the provision of time to discuss and assess experiences and expectations of the world of work and to consider possible career interests and directions, taking into account financial and domestic issues.

The guidance counsellor facilitates the client in the development of an awareness of self, taking into account skills, talents, interests, potential and realistic goals. At some stage this process will involve one-to-one engagement with the client. For some guidance counsellors the relationship with the client continues into employment.

Employment placement

Employment placement involves the guidance counsellor working with clients wishing to enter or re-enter the workplace. The guidance counsellor can undertake a full guidance and advocacy service with these clients.

Employment placement includes a process of engaging with clients to assess personal employment preferences and then working with employers to match recruitment needs to profiles of job seekers. It also involves the guidance counsellor continuing to support clients entering employment. Career and Vocational Guidance and Counselling can involve working with the client in the following areas:

— Career information

— Coping with unemployment

— CV design

— Decision-making and planning skills

— Employment opportunity awareness

— Further and higher educational opportunities

— Job search skills, interview skills etc.

— Psychometric and other relevant testing

— Vocational education and training opportunities

Career and vocational guidance and counselling is a process not a single event. It involves assisting clients to examine their aims and aspirations, to broaden their options, make choices and develop realistic career paths.

Personal Guidance & Counselling

Personal guidance and counselling is an interactive process between counsellor and client which can involve working with the individual in a one-to-one setting or working with the individual within a family or group setting. This process is conducted in a holistic way. Personal guidance and counselling involves facilitating and assisting clients with the following issues:

— Conflict

— Coping with crises

— Coping with transitions

— Cultural

— Decision-making

— Developmental

— Economic

— Emotional

— Promoting and developing personal awareness

— Relationship

— Social

The personal guidance and counselling process aims to help clients to grow in self-knowledge and self-esteem by assisting them to:

— Understand personal emotions, abilities, interests and special aptitudes

— Make and carry out appropriate life choices and plans and achieve satisfactory adjustments in life

Individual Counselling

Counselling denotes a professional relationship between a trained counsellor and a client. This relationship is usually person-to-person, although it may sometimes involve more than two people. It is designed to help clients to understand and clarify their life space, and to learn to reach their self-determined goals through meaningful, well-informed choices and through resolution of problems of an emotional and interpersonal nature.

Individual counselling involves one-to-one sessions between the guidance counsellor and client. A counselling session may involve the following process:

— Clarify the next steps to be taken

— Create a friendly and encouraging atmosphere

— Establish the broad purpose of the session

— Gather information

— Give information

— Identify the needs of the client

— Summarise topics and issues covered during the session

This process should be facilitated using core counselling skills. It is recommended that confidential record-keeping procedures be followed, bearing in mind the requirements under the Freedom of Information Act.

Group Counselling

Group counselling is a broad term covering all types of counselling for more than one person. There are many different ways of facilitating groups but the main premise is that members listen to, support and challenge each other. Thus all the participants learn to listen, communicate and experience how other people see them. The guidance counsellor needs to be aware of the processes taking place within the group and be aware of the impact on each participant.

Individual and group counselling sessions can be useful in assisting clients with decision-making, problem-solving, self-appraisal and development of coping strategies. The following summarises the core aspects of counselling:

Counselling facilitates empowerment of clients, especially those in crisis, by suggesting, exploring and facilitating a range of coping strategies and interventions in a caring and sensitive way appropriate to the individual's needs. Counselling can be successful only in an ethical atmosphere where the client feels secure, accepted and understood, where limited confidentiality is guaranteed and the client is a willing participant.

The overall aim of counselling is to provide clients with opportunities to work in self-defined ways and to live in a more satisfying and resourceful way as individuals and as members of the broader society.

Developmental Programmes

Developmental programmes are designed to assist clients in areas such as social, personal and vocational development. These programmes should aim to assist clients with decision-making, problem solving, behavioural evaluation, transition strategies and the development of coping skills.

Developmental programmes can be delivered in a variety of settings and using a variety of methods to suit individual and group needs. These can include class/group or one-to-one sessions. The use of life skills within the guidance process enables and assists the client to manage transitions from one stage of development to another. Direct involvement in group work enables the guidance counsellor to develop a relationship with individual clients and to identify those who may benefit from individual counselling. Key topics in developmental programmes include the following:

- Assertiveness
- Conflict resolution
- Financial management
- General life-skills
- Goal-setting skills
- Motivation
- Personal development
- Stress management
- Time management

Information Gathering and Dissemination

Information is an important component in adult guidance and counselling. It should inform all aspects of career, vocational and educational opportunity.

Current information is gathered, organized and disseminated to provide the client with as much information as possible on the widest range of options with the goal of enabling the client to make informed career decisions. The effective management of a comprehensive library resource would facilitate the following:

— Access to information technology including Internet and e-mail
— Careers exhibitions
— College open-day visits
— Employment opportunity awareness
— Health related matters
— Helping agencies
— In-depth knowledge of career trends
— Legal rights
— Outreach work
— Research
— Trade unions
— Work-place/industry visits

Information and Communications Technology (ICT)

Information and communications technology is important in enhancing the delivery of an effective adult guidance service. Computers are useful in administering the following:

- College Applications
- *E-guidance (Information and Communication Technologies in Guidance):* The use of e-mail for the delivery of certain aspects of the guidance service
- *Information Retrieval Systems:* These comprise databases of education and training opportunities, occupations and employers
- *Matching Systems*: These involve matching the individual's profile to suitable job opportunities. Matching Systems represent the most commonly used computer applications in the guidance field.
- *Matching Systems:* These involve matching the individual's profile to suitable job opportunities. Matching Systems represent the most commonly used computer applications in the guidance field.
- *Psychometric Tests:* These are mainly on-line adaptations of pencil and paper tests, measuring abilities, aptitudes, personality
- *Self Assessment Profiles:* These are commonly based on an occupational interest inventory questionnaire which should produce a profile in terms of occupational fields
- *World Wide Web:* The Internet offers a wide range of career guidance web-sites covering many career-related areas including job search, C.V. planning and career information.

People generally seek guidance and counselling at times of transition. It is now widely acknowledged that adults face such transition points throughout their lives and often long after they have left the full-time formal education sector. It is also acknowledged that life-long learning requires life-long guidance and counselling. The adult contemplating a new role requires the space and opportunity to evaluate possible options and develop a new career path with a competent professionally trained guidance counsellor to assist and advise.

Re-structured Senior Cycle and the Guidance Counsellor

Some of the implications for guidance and counselling that result from the restructuring of the senior cycle. The contention is that many of the values that underpin the mainstreaming of the Transition Year Programme, the introduction of the Leaving Certificate Vocational Programme and the development of the Leaving Certificate Applied are consistent with a 'guidance' perspective and, consequently, guidance counsellors need to be 'advocates' for these innovations. Furthermore, the altered senior cycle implies a development in understanding of the guidance counsellors's role and presents counsellors with fresh challenges. The 1994 restructuring of the senior cycle has already resulted in some significant changes in the lives of young people. There have also been some important consequences for the professional practitioners who work in schools. As with any major educational innovation, individuals' reactions vary: some embrace the changes enthusiastically, others resist with passion, while the majority seem to get on with their work, adapting to changes, incorporating some aspects of the innovation into existing practice and rejecting others.

The ability to manage change is an essential skill in post-modern society. Change is mandatory, growth is optional. Managing change tends to be easier when some grasp of where the change is coming from and what it means. In a society undergoing rapid economic, social, cultural and political change, the challenge to schools to react to meet new demands is daunting. In the restructured senior cycle, guidance counsellors are presented as critically important people. However, the general rhetoric of policy makers' will only become reality when it is translated into the language of teachers and other professionals in schools. Hence the question arises: what are the implications that arise for guidance counsellors from this restructuring? The perspective offered here is informed by my experiences as a teacher, guidance counsellor, deputy principal and as a member of the support service for the Transition Year Programme.

A New Senior Cycle

The purpose of the restructuring is to provide maximum flexibility in the senior cycle in catering for the different aptitudes, abilities and needs of pupils. All pupils were presented, for the first time, with the possibility of three years in senior cycle. Immediately after the Junior Certificate they could either opt for a Leaving Certificate programme or for a Transition Year. The aims of the optional, additional year at school were defined as fourfold:

- enhancement of general education
- orientation towards the transition from education to life and work.

— remediation and foundation studies and activities

— promotion of greater equity by providing an optional additional year for all pupils.

The purpose of the Transition Year programme was stated as to provide pupils with wider opportunities for personal development'. The restructured Leaving Certificate has three main orientations:

— Established Leaving Certificate, as had been traditionally offered

— Leaving Certificate Applied Programme, 'an option for those who do not wish to proceed directly to third level education or for those students whose needs, aspirations, aptitudes or abilities are not adequately provided for by the other Leaving Certificate programmes.'

— Leaving Certificate Vocational Programme, with the objective of 'enhancement of the vocational dimension within the Leaving Certificate Higher and Ordinary Levels'.

Guidance Context

Significantly, the circular letter heralding the new structures, included a distinct matter headed 'Guidance'. The assertion is that, arising from the new arrangements, pupils will need to acquire information about the various programmes and to 'understand their own abilities, interests and aptitudes so that they can make informed choices between the programmes.

Origins of restructuring

Throughout the nineteen eighties the Curriculum and Examinations Board (CEB) and later the National Council for Curriculum and Assessment (NCCA) proposed greater curriculum variety at senior cycle 'to meet a diversity of interests, aptitudes and needs'. Significantly that view saw guidance and counselling as a key curriculum feature.

Perceptions of the Counsellor's Role

Before looking in detail at aspects of TYP, LCA and LCVP, an examination of perceptions of the guidance and counselling role can contextualise some of the issues that might emerge for an individual counsellor in relation to the new programmes. Departmental circular letters have tended to focus on regulations concerning the appointment of guidance counsellors to schools. The establishment of the National Centre for Guidance in Education (NCGE) in 1995 marked an important development and was an indicator of a growing realisation among policy makers of the potential of the role in schools. The NCGE, along with the Institute of Guidance Counsellors (IGC), have been among the most active players in shaping the role of the counsellor and in identifying boundaries. For example, a NCGE Report to the Minister for Education highlights nine 'important functions' which are seen as the specific responsibility of the Guidance Counsellor. These are:

— counselling
— consultation
— assessment

— information
— classroom guidance activities
— referrals
— vocational preparation
— guidance programme planning
— evaluation of the school's guidance needs and services.

Historical Legacies

The presence of specifically qualified guidance counsellors is relatively recent in Irish schools. From the late 1960s onwards there does not appear to have been a coherent national policy on guidance. Since then it have evolved unevenly and not always in a linear way. In the early days, the tendency was to highlight the role of the guidance counsellor as distinct and individual. Initially, this was necessary because many people inside and outside the education system had a limited understanding of the role. Hence, representative bodies sought to emphasise the unique role of the counsellor. The wider whole school context, seeing the counsellor as a team player cooperating with other professionals was, at times, played down. The severe educational cutbacks of the early nineteen eighties and the very real threat to guidance and counselling—at a time when young people needed the service and student participation at second-level was growing exponentially—further heightened the emphasis on the individual role.

The overall effect was to present the guidance counsellor as engaged in a myriad of tasks.

Comprehensive lists of activities were favoured over attempts to identify priorities. Quantifying the time a counsellor might spend on particular activities was resisted. There are good historical explanations for such an approach. In the early days many guidance counsellors actively resisted too much role clarification in order to highlight the need for flexibility so as to be able to respond appropriately to the varied needs of individual school situations. This lack of clarity also ensured a certain autonomy for the counsellor. The dominant view among counsellors at that time might be summed up as 'trust us as professionals, respect individual differences and let best practice develop'.

There were very real tensions involved in such an approach. There were those, particularly school principals and Department of Education officials as well as some counsellors, who would have preferred more explicit guidelines, even down to how much time might be spent with particular categories of students. It seemed fine to advocate a flexible approach until someone found her/himself timetabled for fifteen hours teaching certificate examination subjects. When such a counsellor tried to negotiate a reduced teaching load, he/she sometimes felt ill-served without a comprehensive job description. Unfortunately, sometimes one of the consequences of such 'negotiation' was that the guidance counsellor was seen, by principal and teachers, as 'uncooperative', 'difficult' or unwilling to engage with full class groups. Within some schools this led to tensions between the counsellor and his/her teaching colleagues. Rather than focus on what the counsellor had in common with fellow professionals on the teaching staff, the tendency was to emphasise the differences.

The threat posed by the cutbacks of the early eighties forced counsellors to present themselves as distinct, even unique among the professional staff of a school. In the eyes of some teachers, this self-definition was seen as exaggerating differences. Tensions sometimes arose and some counsellors retreated, literally and metaphorically, into the relative isolation of their offices. The nature of the student-counsellor relationship and its attendant confidentiality added to the difficulties in some schools. Sometimes, the overall effect was that the counsellor was seen as a specialist, operating in the margins rather than playing a central role in the life of the school.

Principal's Perceptions

There are consequences arising from a loose definition of the guidance role. Some of these emerge in a study of principals' perceptions of the role. However, the lack of clear perceptions didn't prevent school principals from commenting about what they thought school guidance counsellors should be doing with their time.

Counsellor as Collaborator

An emphasis on a collaborative approach to guidance emerges in the 1992 Green Paper :

> While guidance counsellors have a central role to play in this (guidance) process, it is important that the provision of guidance should be seen as a school-wide responsibility, involving the collaboration of the school administration, the guidance counsellor and the other teachers. This direction is made more explicit in the 1996 NCGE Report already mentioned.

For example, in addition to describing the specific responsibility of the guidance counsellor, the 'Responsibility of Schools Management' and the 'Responsibility of the Department' are also outlined. In the mid-nineties the IGC published its own document on the role of the counsellor. This provides some useful overviews and models for looking at guidance and counselling in schools and builds on earlier publications from the IGC on role. It is strong on providing comprehensive lists of possible interventions by a guidance counsellor and consistent with the need for flexibility and sensitivity to different school contexts. As regards the constraints of time, the implication is that individual counsellors and schools have to decide on their own priorities.

At least twelve broad features appear to be distinctive about the three programmes:

— A consistent focus on the personal and social development of students as important educational goals, complementing the established, traditional emphasis on academic achievement 1

— An orientation to and guidance for adult and working life, to be realised particularly through the provision of 'work experience'.

— Learning for citizenship; internationally in the 1990s there was a growing realisation that all democracies need to be nurtured by citizenship education programmes. The Junior Cycle subject Civic, Social and Political Education (CSPE), introduced into all schools in 1997, reflects this trend. The new programmes seek to build on that CSPE foundation.

— An emphasis on self-directed learning and the promotion of 'enterprise'. In a fast changing world where the concept of 'lifelong learning' is gaining currency, 'learning how to learn' is seen as a key skill, as is the ability to take initiatives in new situations.

— The application of active teaching and learning methodologies. The programmes challenge very strongly a traditional passive model of learning. This echoes the National Education Convention's observation: 'the need for styles of pedagogy which engage and involve all pupils more actively in the teaching-learning interaction than was traditional, was realised.'

— Responding creatively to educational disadvantage. All three programmes maintain a focus on the main purpose of the restructuring: to 'provide maximum flexibility in the senior cycle in catering for the different aptitudes, abilities and needs of pupils'.

— Closer links between the school and the local community. The programmes see 'the community' as providing significant learning opportunities beyond the classroom but also reflect a more integrated view of a school's role in community development.

— Innovative forms of assessment. All three programmes indicate that the assessment of student learning should go beyond written, terminal examinations. The thrust of the guidelines is that new forms of assessment can be developed through these programmes.

— The promotion of Informations and Communications Technology (ICT). The guidelines all recognise—with varying emphases—the need to incorporate ICT into teaching and learning as well as its vocational dimension.

— An emphasis on school staffs working cooperatively in planning, delivering and evaluating programmes. This again challenges the traditional culture of many schools, where individual teachers tend to operate in professional isolation from their colleagues.

— Changing relationships between teachers and students. The model of learning implied in the three sets of guidelines is a more 'facilitative' one, closer to the model of learning popular in adult education. The phrase more a guide on the side, than a sage on the stage captures some of the shift in emphasis.

The Guidance Perspective

Many of the common strands in the three senior cycle programmes should, resonate with the guidance counsellor. Counsellors are uniquely positioned to see the need for the shift in emphasis that these three senior cycle programmes represent. They have often listened to young people frustrated with school and realised that the inflexibility of the system was sometimes a bigger stumbling block than the young person's behaviour. Counsellors regularly see the soul-destroying damage to teaching and learning that can arise from an assessment-driven approach. They also see the corrosive effects when stakeholders overestimate the importance of academic learning to the detriment of personal and social development. Working in guidance also gives a unique perspective on how the system's rewards for cognitive/ intellectual aspects of achievement is disproportionate and demotivating for many young people.

On reading the work of Gardner many counsellors quickly identify, from their experience, with his central thesis of people possessing the potential of multiple intelligences working in combination rather than having a single mental capacity called 'intelligence'. And finally, counsellors are familiar with the overwhelmingly positive feedback that sometimes comes from employers about students whose school reports continually suggest mediocrity.

Transition Year Guidelines

In the TYransition Year (TY) programme, guidance should be both integrated into the programme as a whole and treated as a specific component. A guidance programme should be designed to address the needs of all pupils so as to help them to: assess and interpret information related to their abilities, interests, skills and achievements; acquire competences in educational and career exploration and planning; develop knowledge of self and others and of the society in which they live; develop realistic personal, social, educational and vocational goals. The TYP guidelines suggest a core group of four or five teachers to co-ordinate the programme. These should be drawn from distinct curricular areas. This team could, and sometimes does, include a guidance counsellor. The Transition Year Curriculum Support Service in 2000 found that 57.4% of schools had such core teams.

Leaving Certificate Vocational Programme (LCVP)

In relation to LCVP, the guidelines are even more explicit

on how the team should be constructed: In addition to the Co-ordinator, the LCVP team will be drawn from teachers of the link Modules, specialist teachers from the Vocational Subject Groupings, the Guidance Counsellor and teacher/s providing ICT access. Given the emphasis within the LCVP on work experience, on the vocational dimension of Leaving Certificate subjects and on links with community agencies, it is difficult to imagine an effective programme without a significant input from a guidance counsellor.

The Vocational Preparation and Guidance component in the LCA is a major part of the programme and students must complete eight modules. The include guidance, jobsearch, work experience, enterprise, community work and work and living. The guidelines are quite explicit about the Guidance module as it is the only module that requires delivery by a qualified guidance counsellor.

The importance of the Vocational Preparation and Guidance teaching team, working closely with the Guidance Counsellor and the direct role of the Guidance Counsellor, was paramount in supporting students in their work experience.

Of course, even with the school's guidance counsellor installed as a key player within the teams promoting the TYP, LCVP and LCA, there is no guarantee of immediate success. One of the clear messages to emerge from the substantial literature on innovation in education is: expect resistance, especially to implementation.

Challenges for the Counsellor

When the winds of change blow, can be caught between the inclination to build protective walls and the wish to harness the energy by constructing windmills. The changes that flow from the restructured Senior Cycle present counsellors with some very specific challenges. An initial professional responsibility on the guidance counsellor is to be familiar with the innovative programmes, not only the guidelines but also the underlying thinking and the evidence from evaluations. As has been suggested, the guidance counsellor may have a role to play in 'advocacy' within the school, with students, colleagues, the school leadership, parents and outside interests, particularly employers Secondly, there is the need to take stock of current priorities and workloads and re- think them in the light of the evolving changes within schools. At a time of significant change in education, there are implications for all professional identities, including guidance counsellors. The flexibility sought in the early days of guidance and counselling has ensured that a rich variety of practices operate in schools today.

On the other hand there is evidence that such flexibility has led to some stakeholders, including principals, having a limited appreciation of the guidance function. It is difficult to defend the position, apparently adopted by some counsellors, of declining to get involved with the TYP, LCVP or LCA. Many guidance counsellors have adapted and some have shown a keen awareness of the implications of curriculum change for their role. Typically, on foot of the restructured senior cycle, a guidance counsellor might perform significantly in the following ways:

— As a member of one or more programme core-teams, shape the direction of the school's programme to meet perceived students' needs.

— In timetabled classroom sessions, in small groups, and on a one-to-one basis working directly with the students to realise particular programme goals e.g. orientation to adult and working life; personal and social development.

— As an educational counsellor: listening, informing and guiding students around programme and subject choices as well as college courses.

— As an advocate, explaining the rationale for the TYP, LCVP and LCA to other stakeholders. With the development of the School Development Planning Initiative, this dimension of the role may become more crucial.

It is impossible to discuss a shift in role for guidance counsellors without acknowledging the difficult industrial relations situation of recent years. Good quality guidance in schools has always been dependant on significant amounts of good will and generosity of time. When professionals feel undervalued, such additional input becomes vulnerable and cannot be taken for granted.

The development of understandings and perceptions of the role of the guidance counsellor in Irish schools has been uneven. Tensions can exist between a focus on the counsellor as unique individual professional and a more collegial, whole-school approach. To appreciate issues that individual counsellors may have in relation to the restructured senior cycle, an appreciation of the historical evolution of guidance and counselling in Ireland. Teacher development and curriculum development are closely intertwined is also relevant to guidance counsellors. The restructured senior cycle presents guidance counsellors with fresh opportunities to work with colleagues, to engage in meaningful role clarification and to renegotiate priorities with school leaders. Indeed, the invitation is there to significantly reposition the role. This can be seen as part of the wider challenge to ensure that the guidance function within the school remains central rather than marginal.

6

Open and Distance

In the delivery of technical vocational education and training (TVET) through distance education, student support plays the pivotal role. Whether provided to an individual student or group of students, student support is necessary and complementary to the print material supplied. Student support includes all those activities (administrative or academic) which help students progress through the course. Many distance education practitioners have written extensively on the scope of student support in open and distance learning (ODL). They have all emphasised that student support services are integral to the overall working of ODL. And although the objectives of a student support system in distance education cannot be defined as a requirement to guarantee success for all students, it is well documented that when it comes to articulating what we mean by student services, distance educators are way ahead of their colleagues in conventional universities.

Student support in TVET through distance education can be broadly categorised into two areas. The first is the administrative (or non-academic) support and includes activities or services which support students in making enquiries, admissions, pre-study advisory services, record-keeping, information management, non-academic aspects of assessment; library services and other administrative aspects. The second is the academic support, which consists of defining the course, explaining concepts, exploring the course, providing feedback (both formal and informal), providing hands-on practical experiences, developing learning skills, following up students' progress through the course, extending the boundaries of the course and sharing the excitement of learning.

There are a number of approaches followed to provide academic support to students. These include the following:

— Establishing study centres, which are used for tutoring an individual student or a group of students

— Conducting counselling sessions

— Self-study help (peer group)

— Mentoring

— Telephone contact and e-mail

— Television and radio broadcasts

— Specially designed audio-videotapes and computer-mediated communication For hands-on practical work, students are supported either at work (industry based) or at an institution providing necessary infrastructure (institution based). Student support services have to be equitable, gender sensitive and flexible to meet the special needs of learners. The main objective of student support is to support individual learning. It is based on the delivery requirements of clients, not the interests of trainers or providers. The following key characteristics of student support in vocational and professional areas:

— Support should provide a model learning environment.

— Support should build on an existing framework as far as possible and be consonant with the culture in which it is developed.

— Support should be developmental and exploratory, providing experience of a wide variety of teaching and learning opportunities.

— Support should recognise and build on the variety of professional experiences and its participants.

— Support should acknowledge both the private and professional aspects of the learners' experiences and their interconnectedness in the development of learning.

— Support should be rooted in the practical skills development in a real work situation.

Study centres are the backbone of ODL and make it different from correspondence education. A study centre, which provides quality reception and quality tuition to its students, is highly motivating and encourages students to learn. The following support facilities available at study centres:

— A place for individual study in appropriate surroundings and at appropriate times

— Library facilities

— Laboratory and hands-on practical work facilities

— An opportunity for students to meet the distance education institution's administrative staff

— An opportunity to meet fellow students in the same and/or different course

— A focus for students' association activities

— A source of information and guidance to the general public in a local area

— Access to technology

— Access to local guidance and counselling, individual and group tuition, group viewing and listening

— Facilities for taking test and examinations

There can be a great variety in study centres within the same university and also across different open universities worldwide. Here are just a few examples:

— In some open and distance institutions such as Indira Gandhi National Open University of India (IGNOU) about 630 study centres are funded by the institution itself and managed by its full- and part-time staff. Many of these study centres are, however, located in the buildings of other formal colleges. These study centres provide all the functions described above and have a corporate image with which the students can easily identify.

— The other extreme is the model of study centres of Open University in the UK (UKOU). There, study centres are suites of rooms in another institution's building (normally a college of further education), which are rented during evenings or on Saturdays. Students normally attend for face-to-face tuition.

— In Germany and Spain, the communities provide and pay for study centres. These centres are located in community halls, public buildings, town halls and commercial buildings.

— The South African Institute for Distance Education promotes the concept of community learning centres: local community centres sharing their space (and the cost of infrastructure) with a distance education institution. This arrangement allows the distance education institution to get involved in the local community. These study centres are playing a critical role of organising socially significant programmes.

— The Open University of Hong Kong (OUHK) provides facilities for a library, an electronic library, a computer laboratory, a science laboratory, an audiovisual centre, a language laboratory, and places for disabled students. It also provides six self-study centres, study centres, surgeries, television broadcasting workshops, day schools, computers and science labs for hands-on experiments. The Lee Hyson Foundation donated science laboratories and the environmental laboratory, providing hundreds of students at one time with a place to conduct experiments and write examinations. So, unlike the UKOU where students largely conduct experiments independently with the help of home kits, at the OUHK such kits are used at study centres under guided supervision of the tutors.

— The Open University of Israel has the provision of headquarters and about 110 study centres all over the country. Such centres, along with libraries and laboratories, are housed in the conventional education institutions.

— At the Central Radio and Television University (CRTVU) in China, teaching-learning practice is largely through radio and television broadcasts. The university follows a network of provincial radio and television universities (PRTVUs) (governed by the provincial education commissions), branch schools (governed by the civic education bureaus) and TV classes (conducted at workplaces). The network comprises 43 PRTVUs, 666 branch schools, 1100 work stations and over 30,000 TV classes. The core radio and video classes (along with adjunct printed materials) are distributed by the CRTVU, while the PRTVUs are free to develop their own radio and television programmes to meet the provincial education and training needs and to conduct provincial examinations. The branch schools monitor and co-ordinate the teaching-learning activities relating to radio and TV programmes, tutorials, field study, lab work, tests and examinations. They also govern work stations and TV classes. It is the work stations which admit students, distribute materials and conduct tutorials. The TV classes are places to view programmes, conduct hands-on experiments and field studies, and maintain contacts with enterprises/work units to which the students are attached. The CRTVU system is an excellent example of centralised decentralisation and a coherent system of mass distance education and training.

Tutoring

Tutoring brings ODL closer to face-to-face teaching of conventional universities. But skills of tutoring required in distance learning are much more complex and sophisticated than those required in conventional universities. Distance learning promotes independent learning and active participation of the learner: the two fundamental pillars of education. A distance tutor has to perform a combination of the following functions:

— *Defining the scope of the course:* In distance learning, the course materials provided to students define the syllabus. It is, therefore, tutors who define the scope of the course.

— *Explaining the course:* A tutor explains the course through individual tutoring or small group discussions or whole class teaching. The tutor has to be aware of different resources such as audio, videotapes, CD-ROM and other media support available for a particular course that could provide a variety of expositions for understanding the content. Unlike a conventional tutor who provides elucidation of the course, the distance tutor is mindful that elucidation is the responsibility of the course materials and the tutor's responsibility is to facilitate learning. A distant tutor provides alternative explanations when the student seeks assistance on course materials that he or she finds particularly difficult.

— *Developing study skills:* Having strong study skills enables a distant learner to take full advantage of printed and other resources available. The course materials themselves, which are perceived difficult by many students, can't help the students develop study skills necessary to use the materials to their best advantage. Therefore the responsibility of helping students develop those skills falls on the shoulders of the tutors.

— *Assessing students:* In distance education, generally the course material includes a number of self-assessment questions. There are, however, some doubts about their effective use by students. A tutor can informally ask questions to assess students, discuss the answer and frame a supplementary question. Tutors also carry out formal assessment through assignments, which are marked either manually or by computer. Assignments provide an opportunity for invaluable feedback to students. For many students this feedback is the most substantial teaching contact with their tutor.

— *Monitoring progress:* A tutor keeps a record of all assignments submitted by students and takes proactive action if someone seems to be failing in meeting targets.

— *Organising and supervising hands-on practical work.* This function is of special importance in TVET. It is the activity that focuses on the critical skill development. The practical dimension in TVET has led to the development of the concept of partnership between educational institution, industry and community. ODL institutions follow a variety of approaches in providing student support in hands-on practical work. It might be industry-based, where the immediate supervisor of the student or a designated staff person performs the function of tutor for that part of the course. In other cases, the institution offering the course provides facilities for practical work at study centres and/or at its headquarters. The study centre may be specifically set up and managed by the distance learning institution or another conventional institution. At the study centre the faculty members responsible for the course then perform the tutoring role.

Technology and Student Support

Research studies have indicated that student support sustains motivation of students to learn and continue the course and not drop out.

In reviewing technologies that are available for student support in open and distance education, it is tempting to focus on the new and latest developments in information and communications technology (ICT). The experience of open universities in both the developing and developed world suggest that students are best served when a combination of old and new technologies are employed. In discussing the role of technology in student support it is, however, important to recognise that the choices are made in part by what is readily available, what is best for the task at hand, what students can easily use and what is affordable by both the institution and the students.

Audio-based technologies

Radio has long been one of the most important forms of audio technology by many higher education institutions such as University of Nairobi, National Correspondence Institute Tanzania and University of Zambia to support their correspondence courses. Many of the ODL institutions such as Central Radio and Television University of China, Sukhothai Thammathirat Open University of Thailand, Indira Gandhi National Open University in India (IGNOU) and Open University of UK

(UKOU) have used radio for student support. The radio programmes either take up crucial concepts from those covered in the print and clarify them, or they provide an alternative perspective in which to view a concept which is already covered in the printed course material. Radio programmes are not interactive, and they cover only the theoretical part of the course. They do not help in developing hands-on practical skills.

Audio cassettes have been used by almost all institutions providing some form of distance education. Audio cassettes are much more flexible than radio programmes since they can be listened to by students at their convenience. Moreover a student can listen to part or all of a programme on a cassette as many times as he or she wishes. In some countries, audio cassettes are supplementing radio programmes. At the UKOU, the number of hours of radio broadcasts has decreased over the years, but the supply of audio cassettes has increased in the same period. Like radio programmes, audio cassettes also have their limitation in TVET programmes.

Telephone has been used occasionally to offer student support, but telephone support tends to be individualistic and expensive since calls are very expensive in many countries. Telephone support could occur among peers or between student and tutor. One of the advantages of support through telephone is its immediacy. The disadvantage is lack of visual contact and absence of body language. Student support through telephone has the limitation of being restricted to only cognitive aspects of the course, though it has been found to be as effective as face-to-face student support.

Teleconferencing, also known as audio-conferencing, is popular in countries such as Australia, Canada and

India where distances between tutor and student can be great. In this mode, the tutor sets the agenda of the conference and at the other end, which is generally a study centre, a number of students sit across a table with a loudspeaker attached to the telephone. For a conference call to be successful, it has to be structured with the tutor seeking comments from each student by name, rather than from the whole group.

Voice conferencing is the combination of a telephone and computer to provide a complex voice mail service. By making a telephone call to a number set up by the course provider, students can select from a menu of services provided, which can be available even on weekends and holidays. This service has been successfully used in Australia and is on trial at UKOU. One study conducted on students taking law subjects in Australia reported this:

Computer-based voice conferencing system is a potent and cost-effective means of minimising isolation, distance from other students and perceived disadvantages compared to internal students studying same subjects. These bulletins are seen as having a variety of possible uses including covering developments in dynamic disciplines after the cut-off time, extending the "shelf-life" of print-based materials, providing students with particular needs with a valued form of contact and being either a regular feature of subjects or used at peak times. They provide a means for spontaneity and for students to share setting the agenda - features perhaps not often associated with teaching in the distance mode.

Video-based technologies

Television has been widely used by many distance education institutions to support students, particularly in developed countries. Like radio, it reaches a fairly large number of students' homes. Moreover, unlike radio, television programmes permit the richness of full symbolic representation. Developing countries have not been able to use television as much because production costs tend to be higher and broadcasting authorities tend to be reluctant to use air time for small audiences.

Video cassettes are a powerful resource for providing student support in ODL. They do use television, but not the air time. Like audio cassettes, they can be used by students at their convenience, either at home or at the study centres individually or in groups. In TVET programmes, video cassettes play a significant role because they can be used to demonstrate equipment, tools and/or the processes to be used in the tasks being learned. The University of Victoria in Canada used video to support students taking a certificate course in computer-based information systems.

Computer-based technologies

In many countries, computers are being used in a variety of ways to provide student support. Computer conferencing is generally orchestrated by the tutor and involves posting a directional message, like a message on a notice board, which can be accessed by students at their convenience by logging on to a computer either at home or at a study centre. Students can then contribute to the discussion by posting their own messages. They can respond to each other's contributions and the tutor can intervene at any time. In computer conferences the tutor normally takes the role of stimulator and boundary setter. The tutor summarises the discussion at regular intervals and posts more questions for discussion. Studies have indicated that the use of computer conferences is not dependent on prior use of computers and that conferences appeal to inexperienced users. However it is common for students to 'drop out' of computer conferences, so they do need to be supported in the early stages. Learning through computer conference is a self-directed, self-managed and self-motivated process. The students who benefit most from such a system are those who have perseverance and use the conference for interaction and seeking information.

E-mail communication has also become very common. Students use either their own computers or those at a study centres or an Internet café to send e-mail messages to peers or tutors to seek clarification on any topic of the course.

Virtual campuses

A particular development in programme delivery and student support in the last few years has been the establishment of the virtual university or campus, which provides for all transactions in teaching-learning at a distance (from student registration to certification) online. A few independent virtual institutions have arisen in the last decade, and some open universities (like the UKOU) and campus-based universities (like the University of British Columbia in Canada) have aggressively entered the realm of online teaching-learning. The most talked about is the Western Governors University in the US, which employs Internet, e-mail, CCTV, voice mail, audio and video, videoconferencing and postal service for offering competency-based programmes acquired through work and life experiences. Students may use the Internet to download instructional materials and then interact through e-mail. Also, they may meet at a fixed time for interaction through videoconferencing. In both cases the tutor facilitates the interaction. Online libraries and telephone counselling are in place for regular interaction, and the local centres provide for skills assessment, besides e-assessment. There are a variety of approaches that have been successfully used to provide student support in TVET programmes through distance education. No single approach is sufficient to meet varying demands of students and industry. The student support mechanisms have to provide for cognitive as well as psychomotor and attitudinal aspects of learning in TVET programmes. What mode is used by an institution depends on a number of factors including financial and human resources. The technology available to distance education has the potential of providing quality student support required for delivering TVET programmes and has been successfully used by many distance education institutions. The cost of technology can, however, be a constraint on some systems. Innovative and alternative ways will have to be explored.

The Curriculum

A journey to the centre of the process for developing curriculum should find the learner. This has not consistently been the case in academic programme areas, but it has always been common sense and practice in technical and vocational education and training (TVET).

Being learner centred or student centred is a natural orientation in vocational programme development, and since vocational programming has always stressed the process of 'doing,' expressing content in experiential learning terms is a predictable approach. Institutions use a variety of methods to bring learners together in formal and non-formal settings. The traditional method of face-to-face instruction in a classroom and laboratory should allow a curriculum to imitate the workplace, although often this is not the case.

The method of open and distance learning (ODL) should not follow or repeat this error. Instead the method of ODL should mirror the working world and not drastically alter the process of TVET curriculum development. Accept that the end product of TVET is employment for learners, and if accept industry's role in approving the skills that are needed, then use caution in changing the curriculum to meet any method of instruction. It should be clear that this applies to situations where learners are self-employed or where they work for someone else. Care must be taken to identify and sequence occupational competencies needed in the employment world, whether that world is a large company with many employees or a self-employed individual. When industry needs a tradesperson who is skilled in welding two plates of metal together, it should not matter if the training for that skill is conducted at a distance. For training at a distance, however, there are dramatic evolutions in the process of instructional design. Using modern technologies, the educator must carefully choose instructional techniques that will fulfil the curriculum and design an environment where learners can safely learn and practice.

Curriculum development can be described as the process of defining, organising, combining and co-ordinating content so that it leads learners to the acquisition of knowledge, skills and attitudes. For purposes of this discussion, curriculum development is 'what' the student will learn, not 'how' the learning will be accomplished.

Philosophical Approaches

A personal set of values is a major prerequisite that faces each and every educator. From these values the educator must establish and use a personal, philosophical framework, such as behaviourism or humanism, that will guide the process of curriculum development. Selecting this framework is a critical step since it is a reflection of the educator's educational philosophy. In many cases, however, it may be the government or an institution that selects the framework, not the practising educator. Regardless, the framework is derived from learning theories which are linked closely to psychological philosophies. Learning theories are used as a means to explain how learning occurs. It is very difficult for educators to completely agree on learning theories or to build an indestructible case for only choosing one.

Educational learning theories in the 20th century evolved as new theorists adapted and renamed basic concepts. For most practical issues, they can only see the results of an applied response to learning theory. There appears to be at least two main schools of learning theories that are extensively used in TVET: constructivism and outcomes-based approach. The former is emerging while the latter predominates.

Constructivism

Some would argue that there is no knowledge outside of that which gain through experiences. Constructivism holds that learning is the process of applying prior knowledge and experience to a new situation and integrating the new knowledge. Many educators share the view that constructivism calls for the elimination of a standardised curriculum. Rather, it promotes customised curricula and hands—on problem solving. In developing nations, cultural influences and practices can be integrated easily through a constructivist approach. The challenge to curriculum developers becomes how to determine consistency and a common set of standards when each individual is responsible for his or her own knowledge construction. Also, with vocational and technical education, care must be taken to ensure learners are able to do what is desired by employers. Given this dilemma, some might argue that constructivism is better suited to instructional design, as it is more of a process to assist learners to get to the place of knowledge, skills and attitudes than one that defines what is needed. This is especially true when industry specifies what it needs as the end product of education or training.

The second group of learning theories and practices are those expressed in terms of outputs rather than inputs. Grouping them under a generic title, they can be considered outcomes-based. All outcomes-based approaches describe learner performance in observable and measurable terms. Included under an outcomes-based approach is the learning theory known as behaviourism. The outcomes-based approach guides curriculum by setting goals for learners to accomplish. Descriptions of knowledge, skills and attitudes are expressed in terms of what the learner will be able to do. Objectives, such as instructional, behavioural, terminal and performance objectives, are assumed under this approach. Since competence is a critical component of work in business and industry, expressing performance through competencies has emerged to replace objectives. With its practice firmly set in worker performance, TVET programme development is a natural fit for an outcomes-based approach to curriculum development.

A specific example of an outcomes-based approach to curriculum development, Competency-based vocational education (CBVE) focuses on the occupational competencies (skills) learners are expected to achieve, and the performance of those competencies. The following components are usually essential in classifying CBVE:

— The occupational competencies to be achieved by the learner are determined through an analysis of the occupation.

— Learners are aware of the learning outcomes and the methods of assessment.

— Learners are assessed on the competencies by observing their performance in conditions similar to that of the occupations.

There is less agreement on other elements to include in CBVE, such as self-pacing, use of prescribed modules or learning guides, performance checklists and the absolute criteria of mastery. Related knowledge and attitudes should not be separated from the learning of the occupational competencies.

In many cases, CBVE is less concerned with how the competencies are to be learned, and it is possible to use many methods of teaching such as traditional classroom-based, self-paced and distance education.

The processes of developing TVET curriculum has not radically changed, even with technological advances. Individual or group processes are two ways of looking at developing curriculum. A single subject matter expert (SME) can take his or her experiences and put them in an organised display of content. The SME will rely on past experience and knowledge to achieve this result. A small group of subject matter experts could also perform the same task. Working together they may be able to identify areas that might be missed by an expert working alone. An individual or a small group of individuals could also use an interview process to identify the knowledge, skills and attitudes required of the subject matter. Working with subject experts and using a prescribed process of interrogation, a final result can be achieved. Finally, a larger group process, led by a facilitator, can chart the knowledge, skills and attitudes needed to fully describe a curriculum. The results from any or all these processes could be validated by using other experts in the field to substantiate the data.

The Government of India identified the need to upgrade skills in tannery workers to propel the Indian leather industry into the 21st century. The formal education system was unable to meet this need for many reasons: the target group was in the workforce, the numbers to be trained were very large (1.4 million), the areas to be trained were not covered by formal systems, learners were distributed geographically through various tanneries, each tannery had needs specific to local requirements, the educational background of learners varied drastically from graduate to illiterate and tanneries found it difficult to spare workers for training.

The Indira Gandhi National Open University (IGNOU) developed a course which was çompetency— and workplace-based and which used ODL methodologies. Strong partnerships were established between experts both in ODL and in the leather industry to develop and implement the programme. To cater for the range of varied educational backgrounds and languages, the entire course was produced in both print and on audiotape. The delivery system provided support through work demonstration-based training at the worker's tannery, supplementary support through study centres and assistance through partnering institutes located in the community.

Need for skilled training in the leather industry of India standards. A natural product of a well-developed curriculum is a set of standards set by a government or government-appointed regulatory body. Although representatives from industry and education can participate in the standards-setting process, it is important to ensure that they do not exercise a completely self-serving position. Occupational standards describe the knowledge, skills and attitudes needed to perform competently in the workplace. They help business, industry, educators and learners identify the skills needed to succeed. Properly developed, stated and implemented, they will enhance the TVET environment with the following benefits:

— Developing and maintaining a skilled workforce

— Providing an equitable set of benchmarks for accreditation and certification

— Facilitating employee mobility

— Providing assessment and evaluation guidelines

— Providing a means for human resource planning and performance assessment

Essential Skills

Regardless of the philosophical approach used to develop curriculum, employers have increasingly stressed the need for essential skills, also known as employability skills, in the TVET curriculum. These skills must be woven into the curriculum in an integrated fashion. They are important elements in helping people adapt to workplace changes and provide them with a foundation to learn other skills. They are not technical skills, but rather the skills people use to carry out a wide variety of everyday life and occupational tasks. For example, workers in many occupations are required to use writing skills. However, depending on the occupation, the skills will range from filling out simple forms to preparing complex programmes. Some workers fill out simple forms every day, while others write daily or monthly programmes. Improving essential skills enhances a worker's employability. Many different groupings have been designed by various government and industry bodies, but the main ones can be generalised to include the following:

— Computer (information technology)

— Critical thinking

— Lifelong learning (including learning how to learn)

— Numerical (math)

— Planning

— Reading and writing

— Speaking (oral) and listening

— Teamwork

Learning Resources

A well-designed curriculum will lead naturally to the acquisition or development of appropriate learning resources. These may be textbooks that closely match the skills identified. If existing texts do not meet the stated curriculum, specific learning guides or handouts can be prepared. With new publishing technologies, modules developed in this form can be mixed, matched and combined to produce a resource that meets specific design requirements of the curriculum. Computers and new technologies are presenting opportunities to modify the traditional print-based objects into digital components. These components, such as digital audio and video clips, provide alternative strategies for teaching skills at a distance.

Professional development is the ongoing process of increasing an individual's competence. For faculty this includes technical expertise in their field as well as the knowledge and skills to support student learning. Technological changes in the way work is done means that similar changes will be needed in learning how to do the work. Although approaches to curriculum development have not been greatly altered by technology, the skills of teaching have been significantly impacted by it. The need for in-service training has never been greater. Although the learning environment may no longer be a teacher-centred process, teaching skills need to be addressed. Facilitation skills need to be added to the portfolio of techniques. Switching from a face-to-face synchronous environment to a remote asynchronous environment carries a major shift in the approaches needed by faculty. In the end, the need for professional continuing education increases proportionally with the changes in technology that support education.

Access has become one of the most important variables for learners who wish to participate in educational activities. The need for just-in-time training opportunities has propelled ODL as a major tool in providing access to learners in TVET who might otherwise be unable to participate. In many cases, changes to ODL have been responsible for an increase in the demand for education and training opportunities. Although many developing nations lack a sophisticated infrastructure, the pace of technological change in delivering education at a distance is having a positive impact. The technological tools, however, cannot replace sound principles of educational planning and design. This has even greater significance in TVET where safety and demonstrated learning are benchmarks of success. The challenge of replicating the workplace in distance education is less daunting when sound principles of curriculum development are used to analyse the requirements. These principles are aided by a close working partnership of learners, educators, government and employers who support each other to meet all the learning needs. After all, this collaboration merely reflects one of the essential skills required of learners in TVET—teamwork.

7

Strategies in Vocational Education

Creating a new initiative in open learning is an exciting prospect. Traditional technical and vocational institutions are joining a large number of institutions around the world that have recognised that open learning is efficient, effective and provides greater access to quality programmes for more students. The leadership and faculty of traditional institutions want to make a difference. They want to provide greater access to their training programmes. They want to use their scarce fiscal and human resources in the most effective way possible. Open and distance learning can increase their ability to meet that goal. Traditional approaches to the delivery of technical and vocational programmes will continue to be important, and in many instances will be the only way in which certain skills can be imparted; however, increasingly a mix of open learning and face-to-face instruction.

Open learning can teach theory and prepare students to understand the nature of the practical skills they need to acquire. Traditional face-to-face instruction can build on the open learning and provide the hands-on training of practical skills. Adding open and distance learning (ODL) programmes, or including open and distance elements into existing programmes, allows institutions to better realise their mandates. ODL has a long history and around the world practitioners have come to recognise that the application of ODL systems is an effective way to address both basic and continuing training. There is no doubt that demand for training will increase as the complexity and sophistication of the workplace grows. To ensure the skills required of modern economies are available, it is generally recognised that continuous development of the workforce is necessary and must be identified as a basic part of education and training policy. Governments recognise that traditional approaches to the delivery of all education and training needs must be reviewed and that new, more efficient approaches need to be introduced to allow the provision of training within the capability of government to fund it.

Historically, public institutions were slow to adopt ODL methods, but today there are only a few institutions that are unaware of the potential of open learning. For much the 20th century, in locations as separate as Canada and New Zealand, there existed successful record of ODL for technical and vocational education and training (TVET).The private sector has been a strong advocate of open learning for its training programmes, and public institutions have a long and successful record of ODL too.

It is easy to dismiss the notion that ODL can be applied to TVET programmes with focus on hands-on skills. It must be recognised that there are many examples of programmes in the manual skills trades that have been delivered through open learning. Obviously the hands-on training, as has been pointed out elsewhere in this book, must be accommodated in innovative ways. Often the hands-on training is provided through methods such as partnerships with industry and the use of facilities in institutions when students in traditional programmes are not using them. Of course programmes that do not require major practical components lend themselves more readily to delivery through ODL. The Open Polytechnic's BIZ scheme provision has proved extremely popular, mainly because the distance mode allows people to fit their study around the demanding pressures of running or planning their own small business enterprise.

Planning for an ODL Programme

In recent years the advent and convergence of sophisticated computer and communications technologies has spurred the growth of ODL. Technology now allows for significant economies in the development of ODL programmes, and where the networks are available, it adds to the toolbox of the instructional designer. However, sophisticated technology is not essential to the development of an ODL programme, and if it isn't available that shouldn't detract from considering ways to implement programmes to address unmet needs. However, for the practitioner about to embark on developing an institution's first open learning programme, it is important to recognise that these primary and basic elements are the same as for traditional, face-to-face programmes: don't be intimidated by the depth of knowledge about ODL. In many ways it is simply a different way of looking at what traditional institutions already do:

— *Know stakeholders and what is required to satisfy their needs:*The personal support provided by key individuals who will approve programmes, provide budgets or accept graduates. As early as possible it is critical to develop a basis of trust and understanding about what will be done by whom and with whom. Make key stakeholders part of the process; develop in them an interest in a successful outcome.

— *Identify the training need:* There are many ways in which this can be accomplished.

— *Know learners and their abilities:* Once needs are identified, develop a profile of the learners. What is the level of literacy? Are they likely to be self-starters and motivated to complete an independent learning programme? Will they need some assistance in understanding what is expected of them? Can they afford the costs? How will they learn about the programme?

— *Define the curriculum:* The initial programme will be a pilot to assess how an institution might deliver programmes using ODL. A generic topic for which there is likely ample choice of existing distance learning materials would be a sensible initial effort. This initial programme should be one or two courses that address a well-defined need, has support from internal and external stakeholders, and does not require elaborate additional resources for aspects such as hands-on training or an industry placement. Simplicity must be the underlying factor.

— *Ensure student and administrative support systems:* This is an easy area to overlook. Basic systems such as registration and fee collection, examination and student records need to be determined, and the way in which these items will be handled must be carefully considered. The priority must be on utilising the existing institution's systems. Don't waste resources creating parallel special systems.

— *Design a delivery system:* The delivery system must reflect the resources of both the institution and the learner. (There is little point in implementing a state-of-the-art Web-based system if the client group has little or no access to the Internet!) Generally speaking, an initial foray into ODL is best served through a simple delivery system that minimises the possibility of technical failures. This tends to local centres for contact with tutors, pick up and delivery of assignments and instructional materials, mail and telephone communication. More sophistication will be easier to add as initial successes become a base upon which to build additional ODL programmes.

— *Use appropriate instructional design:* Use models that will not intimidate the learner and are suitable to the content. Language levels and cultural context are important if, as is recommended, existing content from another jurisdiction. Any adaptation should ensure that the level and style of language is suitable and that the examples and the context of any illustrative content fits with the local environment.

— *Articulate for credentials:* Of critical importance is the equivalency of the ODL course to existing face-to-face courses that teach the same content. Through the provision of identical credentials, an institution is stating that the ODL programme is not inferior or second rate in comparison with more traditional instruction. It is important that first ODL programme includes this aspect of comparison.

— *Secure and train qualified staff:* Staff with an interest in ODL and who have the necessary academic qualifications should be retained to provide the instructional support. The nature of ODL requires the faculty member to act as a tutor, supporting and assisting the student and grading assignments. The tutor in ODL programmes is not the instructor in the sense that knowledge is imparted. The ODL materials do that. This is an important difference that many instructors new to ODL have difficulty understanding. A carefully designed training programme is required to assist experienced faculty to understand the role of tutor.

The practitioner new to ODL and wanting to implement an open learning programme should keep in mind the issues that have to be addressed are no different from those that need to be addressed in traditional face-to-face institutions. Experienced TVET administrators can easily implement open learning programmes. The skills and experience gained from traditional methods are quite transferable. Those educational leaders who are interested in introducing ODL into a traditional institution should not be afraid to try something. Perhaps, but others have done it. It may not be easy, but, with careful thought and by drawing upon the experience and commonsense of technical and vocational administrators, it is possible to introduce open learning into a traditional institution quickly and effectively.

Start small

Select as the first open learning course to be offered a topic that is small, contained and complete—a course for which there is a large unmet demand and one which will attract a significant number of qualified applicants. In selecting this first course there is no need for an extensive needs analysis. Most TVET administrators are acutely aware of the training needs in the region in which they operate. Pick a sensible option to help get internal support as well as support from external stakeholders.

Keep it simple

More sophisticated courses with practical components can be added as initial entry into open learning proves to be a useful approach to meeting needs. It is important that first course be seen to be successful by more conservative colleagues who probably believe that open learning, while appropriate for academic subjects, has no place in TVET programmes. An important objective is to clearly demonstrate that, although not a replacement for traditional methods, open learning can significantly enhance access to TVET programmes and allow better use of the scarce resources represented by the traditional facility.

Select a team

One person alone cannot create the momentum required to initiate an open learning programme. A tried and true approach is to select a small team of three or four people, without fanfare, to develop the idea and plan for the introduction of the first open learning course. This task force is often called a 'skunk works' and it operates outside the normal structure of the institution, with a clearly defined mandate. It will spend some time understanding what open learning is and is not, and then will proceed to develop a plan to implement a programme.

Three people may be all that is required: perhaps a senior administrator to ensure institutional support, an instructor to ensure content and method appropriate to the subject and the registrar to ensure the student administrative systems are not a problem at implementation time. The team must know what is expected of it. The mandate might be to develop a pilot programmes to determine the efficacy of open learning systems in assisting the institution to meet its mandate. Specifically it might include:

— Selecting a course to be delivered using ODL.

— Selecting suitable content that is available in an open learning format from another institution.

— Determining the degree of adaptation that will be required to deliver acquired content in the local context.

— Determining the structure of the delivery system and the student support services that will be available.

— Determining how the support services might be implemented within current structure and practice.

— Determining the extent and nature of any training that might be required for the staff who will be involved in the initial delivery of an open learning programme.

— Managing the delivery of the initial pilot ODL programme and establishing a neutral evaluation process.

— Designing a feedback mechanism for the first offering to ensure constant monitoring of the systems and their adequacy and efficacy.

— Developing an implementation plan to address issues such as time lines, staffing requirements, student recruitment and articulation issues.

— Developing a budget for the course development or adaptation and the initial offering.

— Defining the critical success factors, around which to build evaluation plans.

— Developing plans for both formative and summative evaluations.

The team must be given the resources and support to do the job. They need to know what that level of commitment is before they begin to work on the programme. Most importantly, a senior administrator must indicate support and act as the champion for the programme to give it the prominence required. This administrator will also reinforce for the team the importance of its task in assisting the institution to develop new ways to better meet its mandate.

Once a plan is in place with necessary approvals and a budget, it is time to offer the open learning programme. Student recruitment is critical to the success of the programme. If the programme to be offered has been carefully selected, there should be a pool of potential applicants to ensure it is oversubscribed. Selection of this cohort is very important. Where possible, steps should be taken to admit students with a good chance of success. It will be very important that the programme be seen as a success, both in terms of the completion rate and the comments of the participants. Success at this stage will allow an open learning programme to grow. If initial foray is not seen to be successful, it may be difficult to try to introduce open learning systems in the future.

With students recruited and the resources in place, the final step is to deliver the program to client group. For this initial offering, a feedback loop from the students into the administrator responsible will be important to allow for any modifications to the delivery services that may be required. Implement evaluation process to allow adjustments as the programme operates. Determine what changes would be appropriate in subsequent open learning programmes. An effective evaluation will also be of great value in promoting the efficacy of open learning programmes to stakeholders.

Teaching Practical Skills

Teaching practical skills is very different from teaching knowledge or theory and it requires some special considerations. Within an educational institution, the learning of practical skills is most often associated with workshops and laboratories, specialist materials and equipment, smaller class sizes and, frequently, longer blocks of time for practice or rehearsal. For the open and distance learning (ODL) environment, the teaching of practical skills poses considerably more difficulties than the teaching of knowledge and theory.

Practical skills means skills performed by hand (as in separating the white and yolk of an egg) or with human intervention using equipment, tools or technology requiring guidance, force or movement (as in welding a joint). Practical skills primarily require physical dexterity, although an understanding of principles, processes and sequences is also essential, especially for more complex practical skills.

In many learning environments, the word "competency" has replaced the term "practical skill." The terms are not entirely interchangeable as competencies can also include the application of knowledge and theory not associated with practical skills. But in general, the demonstration of a practical skill can also be described as demonstrating competency.

Generally both equipment and people are required for the development and assessment of practical skills. The problem is that often limit our thinking in relation to both of these elements.

- — Purpose-built facilities, usually established at enormous expense, have been designed to accommodate the specific requirements of the development, practice and application of practical skills. Multiple sets of equipment or tools required for classroom groupings are expensive to establish and maintain. With the increased use of technology and built-in obsolescence, the shelf life of tools and equipment is reducing and creating enormous pressures on the education budget - a budget that in most places cannot keep up with the expanding demands.
- — The people within the educational environment have most frequently focused on education and training

occurring in institutions with specialist teachers or trainers. This has been particularly so in the development of practical skills. The training of specialist staff remains a focus of teacher training, and industry recruitments into the educational sector have strong affiliations with their particular sector of the industry. As a result the engineering staff haven't ventured into the commercial cookery facilities, for example, and the plumbers certainly have not ventured into the music suites. The creation of specialist training people and facilities has limited our thinking and practice. Need to look to other models that allow us to move in different directions. By creating new models of practice grant learners greater flexibility and increased opportunities while reducing the barriers to their learning.

Learning Practical Skills

Teaching practical skills requires using very precise instructions to enable the learner to follow the process and to repeat the skill. Most often this involves using both visual clues and text or audio prompts. It certainly requires special skills in an instructor if there are no visuals. For open and distance learners, the most frequently used method for teaching practical skills is using print-based illustrations of step-by-step procedures. This method still has its shortcomings, of course, and so alternatives are sought.

A major consideration when teaching practical skills is the diversity in the preferred learning styles of learners. Experiential learners become frustrated sitting through a lengthy explanation of a process; they just want to go and try it out. Theorists need to understand everything in minute detail before they embark on the practical application. Other learners will ask the "what if" questions, and still others will always want to know "why."

Recognising different learning styles is an important factor in assisting learners to develop practical skills. Catering to the different needs is critical for success.

Learning Materials

Print-based materials are a valuable tool in providing instruction for the development of practical skills. Other modes that have more recently overtaken print materials in ODL include video and interactive multimedia on CD-ROM.

Video

While slides and film have been used in the past, more recently video has been the preferred medium. With portable video cameras being readily available and not requiring special lighting or huge production facilities, video is a viable option for many educational institutions. As well, the quality of this technology continues to improve, and the emergence of home video editing suites has reduced its cost. Video editing is a relatively simple process and staff with limited experience can produce a short video without difficulty. While it is not broadcast quality (which remains an expensive business), it is good enough to clearly demonstrate the steps and stages for the processes required to perform the practical skill. It is relatively low cost and can be produced fairly quickly and easily.

Video is a successful medium because it links the audio and the visual together to provide a multisensory experience for the learner. The benefits of video are the ability for the learner to play, replay, pause and rewind to the tape. Because practice and rehearsal is so important in developing competency, video is particularly well placed.

One of the great dangers in using video is that the instructor may decide to include too much information, which can confuse the learner. Learners of practical skills must receive clear and concise directions. The KISS rule (keep it short and simple) is an important first principle to remember with video. A video programme with a maximum length of 10 minutes with several shorter segments is much more useful from the learner's perspective. In fact, recent research with young adults in trade-based courses suggests that segments of less than three minutes are ideal.

Lecturers often struggle with this concept at first as their role in education has been primarily to extend the knowledge of learners by providing explanations and examples. But the longer explanations are best left for a face-to-face setting and not stored on video. The medium dramatically changes the style of educational delivery. While videotapes can be purchased readily in 120- or 180-minute lengths, for educational purposes it is a good idea to avoid these. The longer tapes reduce postal costs and logistical issues relating to storage and control, but frustrate learners who are forever searching for the matter they require. The use of 10- or 15-minute tapes is proving to be a very learner-friendly approach.

CD-ROM

CD-ROMs have the capacity to store a very large amount of information in a variety of formats including text, animations, video, audio, and graphics including photographs, diagrams and drawings. Increasingly three-dimensional representation and simulations are a feature of this technology.

The educational design of CDs is an important feature. It can range from a very basic design, much like a book on screen with page-turning functionality, through to a completely interactive experience. The most critical feature is that the product be learner-friendly and not leave the learner feeling insecure or lost. Clearly, CDs cannot be developed without significant technical skills, and to optimise the learning effectiveness a team approach incorporating a computer programmer, graphic artist, content specialist and instructional designer is the ideal. This raises the issue of cost of development.

The most effective option is to buy an already-developed product rather than go into full-scale production. Economies of scale are important. By using the range of media available, learners can have their learning supported and reinforced in a number of different formats. For example, learners might first view a video, which provides an overview both visually and audibly of the practical skill they are acquiring. The video could be followed by clear digital photographs of the step-by-step procedure with either text prompts or a voice-over to provide additional explanation.

An overview of the complete process could occur in an animation, and then the whole process summarised in dot points using text. This multifaceted approach is particularly attractive because it meets the needs of a variety of different learning styles. The benefits of the CD-ROM format are its capacity to store enormous amounts of information, the range of multimedia that can be incorporated and the cost and ease of replication, distribution and storage. Obviously the technology required to support this approach to teaching practical skills is more advanced and not as readily available as video in most instances.

Online

Online learning is, of course, another creative use of technology in the educational environment. However, this approach needs careful consideration for the teaching and application of practical skills. Extremely good infrastructure is required to enable the use of streaming audio and video, which at present cannot be replicated to the standard established on CD.

Many technical and vocational education and training (TVET) systems are now establishing database-driven clearinghouses to record the availability of learning materials suited to ODL. This enables searches for suitable materials to be conducted more simply. This is particularly important given the proliferation of new materials. Additionally the cost to produce materials is extremely high and it is foolish to undertake such programmes if suitable material already exists. While customisation may be required for some particular cultural or technical reason, it is often better to approach the existing developer rather than try to replicate or customise the resource at great expense.

Learning Environments

In taking a broad look at international developments within ODL, there are a number of trends in learning environments that can be easily adapted to most settings. Consider, for example, self-paced packages for study at home, at work or in community learning environments, as well as the significant move to workplace training. Additionally the emphasis of on-the-job training is on the increase. The focus in all of these approaches is clearly on the learner and his or her learning. It removes the emphasis from the people, facilities and tools, although these are still a major consideration. The development of learning communities or learning partnerships is another significant move in many parts of the world. Based on the concept of lifelong learning, together with the acknowledgement that everyone is a learner and a teacher, exciting new developments enable learning to occur in many different settings. From this perspective, both the community and the workplace are suitable environments to support the teaching and learning of practical skills.

Another trend has been the establishment of mobile classrooms or workshops which allow the movement of facilities, equipment and specialist staff to different locations, although it is restricted to venues linked by suitable transport infrastructure. It allows the teaching of practical skills followed by the assessment of these skills at some future date after practice in the intervening weeks or months.

The development of learning centres (also known as learning commons or information gardens) are an important development in TVET. A community can benefit by supporting a joint educational facility that supports a range of learning outcomes. This may result in a primary and secondary school, technical institute and university combining resources with a local government body to jointly fund a local facility for extended hours of use. In some examples, local industry also accesses the technological infrastructure on a fee-for-service basis to support their own enterprise or small business. This has been particularly successful in close-knit remote rural communities. A co-ordinator facilitates the learning and the use of the facility and oversees the maintenance and upgrades as necessary.

Increasingly partnerships have become a critical feature of the TVET sector, driven by the reforms within the sector that demand closer ties to ensure graduates are employable at the conclusion of their study and that the training is relevant to the industry sector. As highlighted earlier, the increasing cost associated with capital infrastructure, the short shelf life of software, hardware and technology-driven equipment, the diversity in the range of machinery, the variation in processes in competing industries or enterprises and the escalating cost of establishing and maintaining workshops and laboratories are all factors strengthening the need to find new ways of providing training. These include workplace training, on-job training, work-based learning, work experience and the adoption of technology to support self-paced learning in a range of environments. (See chapter 7 for more details on alternative strategies for educational delivery.)

Assessment

It is always important to consider the role of assessment in the learning process. Both formative and summative assessment are critical elements that need careful consideration in the development and design of any learning experience, but never is the design so important as in ODL modes of delivery. In the teaching of practical skills, the assessment must measure the performance of the skill to predetermined standards. Too often a written assessment is devised to test the learner. Clearly there are some styles of questions that will enable a learner to describe their knowledge and skills in relation to practical skills. Most frequently, however, a learner must demonstrate competence by successfully performing the practical skill.

Formative assessment

Formative assessment relates to the practice or rehearsal of the skill. Clearly this requires time for the learner to master more complex skills, especially if a range of performance criteria are a feature of the assessment process. However, many learners are capable of self-assessment during this period if provided with clear guidelines, which limits the role of assessment and increases the role of mentoring during this phase of development. Assessing competence is, therefore, conducted after a period of rehearsal.

Summative assessment

The summative assessment relies on the learner's ability to provide evidence of his or her ability to perform the skills. This assessment may have certain performance criteria attributed to it and therefore speed, degree of accuracy, application under certain circumstances or to predetermined tolerances may be a feature. The learner has to demonstrate his or her ability; however there can be a number of people or environments in which this can occur.

Gathering evidence

Evidence of capacity to perform a practical skill can be gathered in many different ways. Again it is valuable to think beyond the traditional learner-teacher relationship and reflect on using key people and tools associated with the learner. By clearly defining the skill to be performed, learners themselves can give some consideration to how they might provide evidence of their ability.

Sometimes viewing an end product created by learners assesses the demonstration of competency. Without applying the skill it would be impossible for them to complete the task. Alternatively they could record their capability on video by demonstrating the practical skill. This method requires additional human and physical resources and is not always feasible or practical. Other examples use validators to verify that learners in an industry or community setting display the skill. Feedback from an employer, supervisor, customer or peer is a useful measure in gathering evidence. An alternative to workplace assessment that supports learning at home or in the workplace is the approach that allows the learner to learn in an environment that suits his or her needs and then requires him or her to attend an assessment centre. This may be a local venue, technical institution or other community facility which has a suitably qualified assessor as well as the equipment required to enable the learners to demonstrate their practical skills.

Workplace trainers and assessors

One approach gaining wide acceptance is the use of workplace trainers and workplace assessors. Many individuals will have both qualifications while others may only concentrate on the assessment role. Workplace trainers and assessors are most often existing employees with higher level skills who oversee the learning of staff in the workplace. They are frequently the supervisors of employees who are developing or upgrading their skills base. Workplace trainers and assessors must complete a training programme to understand the essential elements of learning and assessment. Once qualified, they support learners and the learning process within the workplace. Workplace trainers and assessors perform their tasks on behalf of the certifying training organisation. Maintenance of standards and quality assurance issues therefore remain the responsibility of the certifying body, which is important to preserve the integrity of the qualifications being issued.

With this model there is a major investment required in human capital, course development and training for the implementation of a model based on workplace training and assessment. However this approach does have many benefits in terms of building a strong training culture within industry and in reducing the replication of expensive public education facilities and infrastructure.

The recognition of current competence (RCC), otherwise known as the recognition of prior learning (RPL), is a feature around which entire pre-assessment centres are now being established. This approach acknowledges that many learners come to a course of study with existing knowledge or skills. For others, their life or work experiences may have provided them with all the skills required for certification at one or more levels, yet they may have been denied the opportunity for formal study and recognition of their skill base.

RCC is a useful tool to acknowledge the skill base in a community or workplace and establishes the credibility of skilled individuals, who may have formerly been untrained or unqualified, to provide a supervisory or validatory role in the learning experience. It requires the demonstration or evidence of practical skills in some form for assessment purposes.

In considering the role of teaching practical skill development in ODL, there are a number of issues that must be carefully considered. Clearly there is a need for learners to follow instruction, to practise and to demonstrate their competence where the learning of practical skills is involved. This will always require the support of skilled people and a range of tools or equipment to enable the skill development. However, more and more creative approaches to practical skills development are emerging and most can be adapted to local settings.

The emergence of new models for educational delivery and assessment is increasing the learning opportunities. These more flexible approaches frequently involve joint partnerships with industry or community entities, but the benefits for the learner, the employer and the training provider generally outweigh the complexity of the arrangements.

Considerable thought must go into the adoption of many of these models as the initial set-up requires considerable capital investment. What is not frequently understood is the need for ongoing capital as technology is a consumable because of its built-in obsolescence.

The use of public funds to encourage a training culture within industry and a collaborative approach to the use of industry standard equipment and facilities, which reduces demand for public resources to duplicate workplace environments, are fundamental issues to be addressed when considering limited education budgets. The movement of resources to empower different people and facilities to be accessible for training opportunities is a feature which needs careful consideration by policy-makers. Without a doubt, the commitment to educational resources, especially educational technology to support ODL, must also be a high priority. The strategic use of these resources is a major consideration and a closer analysis of the particular options is critical. By focusing on the learner and the learning outcomes, educationalists can significantly reduce the barriers and increase the opportunities and flexibility offered to their customers.

Delivering the Programme

If access to technical and vocational education and training (TVET) is to increase, new ways of developing and delivering courses must be explored. TVET must be taken outside of the classroom and into the communities, the workplaces and the homes of the students. Traditional ways of thinking about TVET must be put aside and different ways of packaging and delivering knowledge and skills must be developed. This is particularly critical in meeting the demands of countries with depressed economies and countries where people are separated by water (as in island states), by terrain or by distance.

Different approaches to learning allow learners a greater say in what, where, how and when they study. These flexible approaches are based on some form of open and distance learning (ODL) methodology which allows learners to study from home, work or a community facility. This off-campus approach is fully supported with materials and contact with a resource person, and may include the following components:

— Self-paced learning packages, which are interactive written materials enabling learners to work individually at their own pace. These packages are often supplemented with audio or videotapes and CD-ROMs. They may be used on or off campus.

— Mixed-mode study, which involves the above approach combined with workshops, tutorials and other structured activities.

— Online delivery, which provides computer-based learning materials via the Internet.

This technology also allows the learner to interact with other students and staff through the use of e-mail and computer chat sessions.

— Videoconferencing, which allows learners to attend a convenient and suitably equipped location and participate in a class at another location. This reduces the time and resources that the learner may need to commit in travelling to classes.

— Audioconferencing, which uses the telephone as the basis for communicating with learning. This is usually used in conjunction with self-paced materials. By repackaging knowledge and skills, using print-based learning materials supported by audio, video and CD-ROM or by on-line delivery, which has severely constrained access to TVET for a number of years.

Adoption Technology

Those who develop trade-based programmes face the dilemma of finding efficient ways of teaching their learners. Teaching practical skills is an essential component in many of the traditional trade areas, and it has generally occurred by demonstrating these skills to the learners by an experienced lecturer in a workshop setting. New approaches are slowly emerging.

Embracing information and communication technology (ICT) provides yet another model for learning. Online learning is being promoted in almost every educational system in the western world. By utilising the Internet, students can study anywhere, anytime provided they can log on to a computer that is connected to the World Wide Web. Within the educational sector this phenomenon is attracting huge attention, and millions of dollars are being spent developing suitable resources. There are, of course, some real benefits and major considerations to think about before adopting this approach. The cost and reliability of the infrastructure are critical factors. Computers simply become consumables within the budget needing to be replaced every 18 months to two years. An unreliable service is very frustrating for learners and can result in many of them leaving the programme discontented. Developing specific online material is extremely costly and the staff development is very time intensive. The rate of development in this field is massive with new supporting software, systems and associated skills turning over in increasingly rapid lifecycles. Research now indicates that online learning may not be quite as big as first thought, recognising that it is not always the most suitable approach to learning and that a blended approach may be more realistic. E-learning has its place within the range of options available. Its limitations include difficulties with streaming audio and video; with less than optimum infrastructure and slower computers, content looks very much like text on the screen. It has been documented that learners read 25% slower from the screen than from print-based materials, so text on screen is a poor substitute. Additionally it can be very expensive for learners if they are required to print materials from within their package or connect to the Internet through an Internet service provider (ISP) sometimes at very high payment rates.

Another pilot programme has had extremely good results using interactive CD-ROMs. This approach produced the following benefits:

— Benefits to the employer

— Decreased time taken to complete the units of up to 50% over traditional methodology

— Decreased time the learner is away from the business

— Greater flexibility in the times when apprentices may attend for practical skills training

— Benefits to the learners

— Learners work through the learning materials at their own pace

— Increased learning effectiveness

— An increase of 20% in the successful completion rate

— Learners who are sick or who miss a matter can easily catch up using the learning materials at home or work

— Learners can repeat a matter many times if they find a concept or practice difficult to grasp

— More leraners can access the tutorial materials

— Benefits to the training provider

— An increase of 20% in the results achieved

— Lecturers are freed up to spend more time with students who need additional help

— Less equipment is required.

Flexible learning - anywhere, any place, any time

There are many areas of training within the scope of TVET that can be offered anywhere, any place, any time. Courses can be developed to meet the particular needs of the target group of students and then delivered to those students in a way that meets their cultural needs, at a time and place that suits the demands of their lifestyles. Often ways can be found to overcome remoteness, low levels of literacy and lack of access to traditional educational facilities. This requires a creative approach, an assessment of the available resources and an ability to harness these resources.

The development of learning centres is important to increase access to TVET. A community can benefit by supporting a joint educational facility that supports a range of learning outcomes. This may result in a primary and secondary school, TVET Institute and university combining resources with a local government body to jointly fund a local facility for extended hours of use. In some examples local industries also access the technological infrastructure on a fee-for-service basis to support their own enterprise or small business. This has been particularly successful in close-knit remote rural communities. A co-ordinator facilitates the learning across all sectors and oversees the maintenance and upgrades as necessary.

Another model gaining wide acceptance is that of workplace training, where training is modelled around existing work activities and related problems. This may involve complex activities and learning a wide range of knowledge and practical skills that relate to the activity, but not frequently associated in a single module of study. Again this requires partnerships within industry or commercial businesses. It may be supported by workplace trainers and assessors or managed by supervisors with customised resources developed by educational staff. This approach is extremely valuable for shift workers who have traditionally been denied training opportunities.

— Benefits to the employer

— Staff do not have to leave the workplace to learn, reducing travel costs and inconvenience

— Staff undertake the study at times convenient to the business

— Training is easily customised to suit the needs of the particular company

— Benefits to the learners

— A culture of lifelong learning is established within the industry

— Learners uses the industry-standard equipment and specialty equipment required in their workplace

— Learners are supported by work colleagues and an educational expert

— Lecturer may be only a phone call away and checks in regularly

— Excellent learning materials are available

— Benefits to the training organisation

— Reduced infrastructure required

— Reduced direct input from the teacher

— Partnerships with industry enable access to all necessary equipment for video development without capital outlay

— Greater access to learners as geography is no longer a barrier

— Processes for managing learners and learning are streamlined

— Material costs and maintenance budgets are diminished

Another approach to learning practical skills is a work experience programme. Again this relies on partnerships with industry or enterprises, but it allows individuals to assess their potential to meet the requirements of a particular job or role. Work experience programmes are used extensively in senior secondary or general vocational courses to assist learners to decide on a stream for their vocation. It allows them to work, for no monetary benefits for an agreed time, usually one week, to gain a fuller understanding of the range of skills and personal attributes required for the position. During this time some training occurs, covering basic practical skills. This is a more general approach and rarely links to formal skill assessment, but it does generate skills that may then be recognised within a future training programme.

Mixed-mode or a blended approach to learning is gaining wide acceptance within TVET. The trend to integrate differing approaches to suit the needs of the learners and increase their access to TVET is critical. It is important that this learner-centred culture is established within the TVET sector. Flexible approaches to delivering learning must be an integral part of the educational infrastructure, not an optional extra. Not only does this approach require different strategies for implementation and the deployment of significantly different policies and practices across entire systems and within TVET organisations, it requires different relationships with the learners. Consideration of the availability of learning materials, existing or accessible infrastructure and trained human resources to support the learning are all vital in re-engineering approaches to educational delivery. Alongside this is the very real need to ensure TVET staff are aware of the changing approach and to support the implementation of new strategies with suitable professional development.

8

Methods of Vocational Education

Although an international comparison of macromodels of technical and vocational education reveals major differences, the didactic micromodels chosen by different societies to impart those occupational skills that are considered necessary are very similar. The differences between these models can best be evaluated when the models are examined in practice to see how they work and prove their worth in modern industrial production and services.

Occupational competence is acquired by learning, in an occupational setting, to work in a manner integrating different problem solutions in a systematic way. These learning processes include in particular:

— Process learning -the mastery of techniques and processes to acquire technical competence;

— Social learning—the mastery of social processes in the workplace and in the enterprise to acquire social competence;

— Learning to plan—the mastery of target-oriented integration of techniques and processes, social processes and skill utilization to acquire planning competence.

Process learning

Competence at work consists in mastering a few basic techniques which are integrated with the required tools, materials and substances so as to achieve, by way of a number of operations, the goals set.

Examples of basic techniques from the occupational field of metalworking to be mastered in theory and practice are:

— measuring, calibration, gauging and marking technology;

— cold-working and hot-working (e.g. bending);

— cutting (e.g. sawing, drilling, turning);

— joining techniques (e.g. friction-type locking and positive joining, such as threading, riveting, welding;

— controlling (e.g. feed motions at machine tools).

Social learning

Systematic work cannot be effective unless it is integrated into the existing formal and informal social processes in a enterprise. This is why social learning must address above all the social processes in the environment of the workplace; it must include in particular

— the horizontal (colleagues) and vertical social processes (cooperation at work);

— the handling of structural and behavioural influences as well as conflict settlement and its techniques (conflict settlement);

— the management structure and flow organization of an enterprise (work organization).

Learning to plan

Desired occupational problem solutions (performance of jobs in the enterprise) are possible only by means of target-oriented, planned integration, in particular

— of the various techniques and processes;

— of the various social processes.

The ability to bring about such integration systematically is termed planning competence; this competence can help to integrate the following individual processes:

— the various techniques and processes (e.g. sawing, welding);

— the various workplaces (e.g. bench, machine, assembly line, individual and group workplaces, operational · logistics);

— the various (horizontal and vertical) social relations;

— the various management and administrative functions within the enterprise (job scheduling, job evaluation, · accounting, works council, insurance and health);

— the various communication systems (linguistic, mathematical, graphic as well as electronic communication);

— the various utilization systems (enterprise and market).

Didactic Models

The purpose of a didactic model is to assist in the organized acquisition of occupational skills required for the reproduction and development of society and economy (social and economic function) as well as in the creation of permanent employment opportunities for those who have completed initial technical and vocational education (individual and social function).

Criteria for the selection of learning goals Didactic models are determined in the first place by their learning goals, which guide them and which describe their learning level and rank. The selection of learning goals can be based on the following criteria:

— reproduction, i.e. the mastery of perfect application of the techniques learned;

— polyvalence, i.e. the mastery of techniques as well as social and planning processes via theory-guided, integrated occupational activities in occupational fields;

— autonomy, i.e. the mastery of techniques as well as social, utilization and planning processes via theory-guided, integrated autonomous activities in occupational fields.

The learning goals always has an economic aspect, too, because the application of these goals has to take account also of the organizational and financial conditions prevailing in a country. The selection of didactic models has to take account of the following economic criteria:

— time economy, i.e. the optimization of learning and examination periods;

— material economy, i.e. the optimization of material utilization, maintenance and repair, self-supply, economy, recycling;

— staff economy, i.e. the optimization of the use of teaching staff, counsellors, curriculum experts, members of examination boards;

— space and equipment economy, i.e. the optimization of the use of buildings, equipment, boarding schools, of traffic and maintenance costs pertaining to central institutions of technical and vocational education.

The learning contents to design and structure curricula, which must be based on learning goals, must ensure that the curricula become compulsory for a whole country, a region, a school type, an occupational field or a subject, if general goals of social policy in its widest sense are to be pursued. The claim to a general validity of curricula is based on specific criteria:

— standardizability, i.e. learning goals, curricula, learning periods, examination level, the specific abilities of the teaching staff and material constraints (learning aids, school buildings) must be described in a standardized way;

— reproducibility, i.e. the standards described must be applicable to any given place of learning, by any teacher or instructor, at any locality, and at any given time;

— quantitative adjustability, i.e. the learning standards mentioned above must be adjustable according to quantity, depending on a desired enhancement or reduction of goals;

— transferability, i.e. the standards described above must be transferable according to specific sociocultural conditions (e.g. in the Third World, in various regions of a country) without the need to abandon principles and criteria.

The purpose of didactic models is to impart the qualifications considered necessary by society; the organization of the models answers the question where and how occupational competence is to be acquired according to well-defined learning goals. A comparison of the different structures developed in industrial societies for imparting working skills shows that, basically, only four clearly distinguishable didactic models of the organization of vocational education exist:

On-the-job training

On-the-job training is the oldest and most frequent (natural) type of technical and vocational education in all societies and, in its pure form, has the following features:

— *Organization of learning:* The trainee acquires skills in the enterprise by observing, imitating, joining in, assisting and trying, by informal imitation of what he or she sees. Working on real jobs in the enterprise makes immediate economic sense: The products which the trainee has helped to produce reach the market, and their quality is controlled by feedback provided by the demand for such products within the enterprise and at the workplace. The trainee's work is always practical, at all times related to real demand, and it provides the prerequisite for the trainee's future ability to earn a living. The trainee shares the communicative, social and ritual relations within the community of staff members, which has its own spirit and will influence the trainee's way of speaking, behaving and thinking.

— *Teaching staff:* The professionally competent master craftsman, the journeyman, the experienced coworker take over work tasks required by the market, negotiates with clients, with the customers' department or the job scheduling department in the enterprise, he passes on appropriate tasks to the trainee, he plans the work and work processes, in many cases he joins in the work himself, he instructs the trainee, e.g. by way of the four-stage method (preparation, demonstration, imitation, practice), he controls work progress and evaluates work results; in short, it is the teaching staff's task to make decisions, to give or refuse permission, to instruct, to assure, to evaluate results, to settle conflicts, etc.

A critique of on-the-job training from the point of view of technical and vocational education theory The description of ideal on-the-job training raises the question why this traditional form of vocational education is being replaced partly or wholly by artificial, school-based or quasi-school systems (e.g. a basic metalworking course in a training workshop or in part-time vocational school).

Criticism of on-the-job training from the point of view of technical and vocational education theory has a long tradition. The complete or partial shifting of vocational education to systems outside real work situations as a result of this criticism cannot be explained solely by the gradual social development of certain life styles, tasks and roles (e.g. the transition from sick-care at home to the modern hospital system); rather this shifting has been caused by the conflicting aims of company management and modern learning. The following factors are important in particular:

— The company, with its management and technological structure, is designed to optimize goods production with the aim of complying with the competitive conditions presented by the market; the company's structure has not been developed to meet the requirements of vocational education.

— The company depends for orders on the market situation and thus on an accidental segment of goods production (specialization), the possible result being merely segmental opportunities for learning against the demand for a complete set of learning goals.

— The company employs its staff as goods producers, for whom the teaching of young workers can be no more than a side occupation.

— The company is exposed to the market's continuous pressures for modernization and develops new and ever more complex structures with the result that vocational education becomes more and more marginal.

In response to the criticism voiced by vocational educationists, attempts were made to overcome the structural weaknesses of on-the-job training by introducing didactic systems that either supplement on-the-job training (part-time vocational school, introduction of systematic models like MES, courses in the framework of intercompany training) or replace it. These systems must be described explicitly as non-direct forms of learning. All known didactic structures are, however, characterized by the claim that they undertake to imitate and approximate real work situations in the · company.

Artificial didactic systems which expressly strive to supplement or replace on-the-job training are based on the following considerations:

— *Place of learning:* Vocational education in this framework must take place in a separate place of learning explicitly reserved for vocational education, for example in training workshops, training laboratories, vocational schools, intercompany training facilities, etc.).

— *Organization of learning:* The corporate structures which by definition aim at production and prevalence on the market do not allow systematic learning which is in keeping with the approach recommended by technical and vocational education theory. Specifically designed didactic systems, on the other hand, are based on systematic learning processes adhering to the laws governing learning. In order to support learning, systematic teaching aids are used (textbooks and tables, laboratory devices, audiovisual aids, etc.), the express purpose being that learning goals (such as learning targets, curricula) are achieved, learning times are optimized and, in particular, trainees are made to understand technological, scientific and mathematical laws involved in the jobs they perform.

— *Teaching staff:* Didactic planning, instruction and the control of learning progress in technical and vocational education are the responsibility of full-time teaching staff, who have been specifically prepared for this task through their own work experience and through familiarization with technical and vocational education theory; their work is based on the results of systematic research in technical and vocational education.

Whenever societies decide to supplement or replace traditional on-the-job learning with alternative types of training, artificial systems emerge which have been designed explicitly for the purpose of technical and vocational education at a specific place of learning. This decision is roughly subject to the following criteria:

Course instruction

Industrialized societies have developed a methodological approach which is the opposite to on-the-job training: course instruction. This method is based on a so-called basic metalworking course developed during the late nineteenth century, and since then has been introduced in company-based training centres, vocational schools and -intercompany or other off-plant training centres, with its basic methodological structure unchanged. Course instruction has the following characteristics:

— *Place of learning:* Course instruction requires for its implementation a specific place, separate from real work situations in the enterprise, with specific jobs to be learned, e.g. of basic technical and vocational education; of an introduction to welding, hydraulics and pneumatics as well as for CNC technology.

— *Organization of learning:* The complex and usually integrated work skills to be learned in the enterprise and later to be applied in real work situations are broken down into a series of individual learning units and practice periods, organized by degrees of difficulty (progressing from easy to difficult jobs and from simple to complex tasks); they have to be mastered by the student in a linear and additive manner, progressing from one training phase to the next. A great variety of highly developed learning aids are used to ensure didactic planning, imparting of knowledge, and control of learning progress. Experience gained in course instruction has shown that breaking down complex jobs into sequences is likely to lead to a high level of performance of students within relatively short training periods. As a result of this favourable experience, this approach was adopted also for other occupational fields (e.g. electrical engineering, building and wood engineering, plastics technology, printing technology, textile technology), including also theoretical instruction (subjects, courses).

The great advantages of course instruction, i.e. breakdown into sequences, polyvalence, transparence and its regular nature, have contributed to the extraordinary spread of this teaching method initially in Europe and later in the United States, and also in technical and vocational education in the developing countries, for it has been found that course instruction can be adapted with relative ease to all societies, cultures and languages. Another achievement in technical and vocational education theory is the polyvalent learning structure; course instruction helps at the same time to overcome the traditional principle of training in a single occupation by preparing students instead for a variety of related occupations and activities, so that they are flexible enough to handle unfamiliar, unforeseeable tasks as they arise.

The introduction of simultaneous, supplementary instruction in theoretical subjects at in-company schools or public vocational schools has turned out to be yet another consequence of course instruction with its strong emphasis on process learning (acquisition of work practice).

— *Teaching staff:* The temporary or permanent separation of vocational training from the enterprise, combined with the construction of specific artificial systems of learning (as in course instruction), calls for teaching staff who are acquainted with the teaching methods required for this task; the result is that there is a need for special training facilities for instructors and teachers at vocational schools, combined with research in technical and vocational education theory on the part of trade associations, at institutes and at universities.

In course instruction, teaching staff can rely on well-proven learning aids in order to prepare and support instruction and to evaluate learning results. The whole learning structure is highly independent of the individual teacher and ensures fair evaluation; this is why long and costly training of the teaching staff is unnecessary. In this case it is sufficient to familiarize the staff with relevant teaching methods, provided that they have successfully carried out their occupation for some time.

A critique of course instruction from the point of view of technical and vocational education theory

— *Place of learning :* The advantages of course instruction are obvious; they can, however, become counterproductive if learning at a separate place of learning (which is necessarily simulative) loses contact with the real work situations in the company because it takes place outside the company for too long. How long it is advisable to have training outside the company at a separate place of learning depends on the structure of big enterprises with a high degree of rationalization and a specific company size (e.g. in motor vehicle construction, in the steel and chemical industries), which demands that vocational education be separated wholly or partly from real work; the structure of small and medium-sized enterprises under increasing pressure for specialization, which forces these enterprises to provide vocational education, at least partly, outside the company (e.g. in part-time vocational schools and in intercompany vocational education facilities) if the said learning goals are to be achieved; the structure of the trainees, which means that high-achieving, confident and creative trainees learn more easily in real work situations than lower-achieving individuals who need more attention and sustained support; the structure of the learning contents, which means that learning contents with a major theory component (i.e. in electronic engineering, in natural science occupations) are with advantage taught in special places of learning, while others with a major experience and practice component (e.g. in mechanical engineering) are preferably conveyed in real work situations.

— *Organization of learning* Didactic systems with a linear structure can become counterproductive whenever the entire didactic system of a place of learning is dominated by rigidly fixed learning sequences, by an isolated learning situation, and above all by the expected results of learning; in this way both the complexity of real work situations and the complexity of occupational problem solving processes are sacrificed while, really, this is what vocational education should, deliberately and systematically, convey.

Learning goals which go beyond the mastery of normal work processes—for example theory-guided and autonomous action - cannot be realized in closed didactic systems with a high degree of outside determination by teaching staff.

— *Teaching staff:* It is a law inherent in social groups - in this case instructors and teachers of vocational schools - that these groups develop for themselves collective interests (and bodies representing these interests), which can also become counterproductive by undermining the mandate of vocational education; this is true whenever status and income considerations are given preference over the vocational mandate and the pertinent continuing education.

An alternative method which is clearly different from course instruction, i.e. programme instruction, has been successfully developed with the explicit aim of overcoming the latter's weaknesses.

— *Place of learning:* For this teaching method, too, it is necessary to have a location for training which is separate from the real work situation, because otherwise the extensive planning effort required for programme instruction is impossible to make. On the other hand, however, the selection of programme tasks taken from the manufacturing process, and reintegrated into this process on completion of the programme, provides interesting possibilities for teaching. At the time of shifting from course instruction to programme instruction or of an enhancement of course instruction by programme instruction, new requirements emerge for the relevant training institution. This is true in particular for the equipment and the organization of workshops and laboratories, which must make programme solutions possible.

— *Organization of learning* :The purpose of programme instruction is to imitate the complexity. of real work in the enterprise by simulative learning which is close to reality, with the aim of avoiding the remoteness from reality which is characteristic of course instruction.

The selection criteria for programme instruction are expressly oriented to polyvalent and autonomous learning; this means that the organization of learning must be based on autonomous problem-solving on the part of the students. Instruction focuses on jobs which have been selected according to economic and didactic criteria and which must allow the integration of techniques, social processes and planning processes; in terms of the degree of difficulty, enable students to produce problem solutions on their own initiative; by way of their function, possess a practical value (if possible with social relevance) in order to make sense for the student and be likely to be completed within a foreseeable period of time and at reasonable costs.

In contrast to the predetermined learning structure of course instruction, programme instruction must proceed from an open learning structure, because learning processes and learning results cannot always be planned.

The risk of failure must be explicitly accepted. The learning processes, which are not precisely calculable as a result of the largely autonomous learning on the part of the student, can be made visible by previous and subsequent courses, the aim being to ensure near-complete achievement of the said goals of learning.

— *Teaching staff:* In contrast to course instruction, which is based on precise rules and regulations, programme instruction makes great demands on teaching staff in terms of planning, implementation and assurance of the results of training. Preparation of instruction requires a great deal of time, imagination as regards the anticipation of possible events, and great commitment including the readiness to deal with conflicts emerging with the students.

A critique of course instruction from the point of view of technical and vocational education theory. The fact that programme instruction in technical and vocational education (and also in general schools) has hitherto made only slow progress has important reasons:

— *Place of learning:* The redesign of the places of learning in order to make them suitable for programme instruction is expensive; as a rule, more floor space is required to provide room for learning groups to move about, a new arrangement of work benches and machinery for group work must be introduced (e.g. pentangular benches, combination benches, mobile machinery) and traditional machine rooms must be variable. Places of learning for integrative learning of theory and practice and new learning aids must be created; on the whole, this means complicated and costly investment.

— *Organization of learning* :In particular, a desirable 'open' learning structure which is not predetermined for every situation that may arise has traditionally not been regarded as guaranteeing the success of training. Since learning processes cannot be planned precisely, considerable structural conflicts and social disturbances are bound to occur and, above all, learning goals cannot be controlled and guaranteed as in course instruction and in subject-related vocational school instruction.

Learning in school-run enterprises

The expression school-run enterprise is liable to misunderstandings, because it is open to at least two different interpretations:

— *First interpretation* : School-run enterprises are explicitly organizational, economic and didactic models which link technical and vocational education to production for the market; the manufactured products and the production processes are used for vocational education and students are allowed to work for production as they acquire more skills.

— *Second interpretation:* Other didactic systems, too, including course and programme instruction, allow students implicitly to fulfil production tasks for the market. The production tasks to be completed contribute to vocational education, and the students are allowed to work for production as they acquire more skills.

For clarity's sake, it is suggested that only the first interpretation of school-run enterprises should be accepted, and that the second interpretation should better be explained with the expression "learning by carrying out production tasks". The following thoughts therefore relate to the first interpretation, i.e. an explicitly organized school-run enterprise.

— *Place of learning:* School run enterprises are separate training institutions, which, though similar in equipment to the manufacturing plant, are, in addition, supplied with all necessary equipment for teaching and learning (classrooms, laboratories, media rooms, etc.).

— *Organization of learning* The organization of vocational education is structured in such a way that all previously discussed teaching systems can be linked consecutively with one another. Safeguarding this didactic model is possible by an external partnership cooperation with neighbouring enterprises, with local and regional markets, with schools in the general education system, and with the institutions of continuing technical and vocational education. The definition of a school-run enterprise includes the following characteristics:

— *Procurement:* For manufacturing and vocational education it is necessary to make products which have sales chances on a local or regional market; cooperation with neighbouring enterprises is expedient; this is true in particular of the procurement of materials, of the modernization of technical equipment and of the recruitment of teaching staff.

— *Manufacturing:* The selection of work tasks also takes account of the occupational skills of the students. This is why, in order to optimize learning opportunities, preference is given to labour-intensive tasks (prototypes, devices, repair, maintenance, etc.). Mass production is justifiable in school-run enterprises only as a planning task.

— *Selling:* Goods produced are sold either by the school or by partner enterprises or by special selling agencies.

— *Funding :* The proceeds from the sale of products, from remunerated work in continuing education and from innovation counselling, provide some relief for the school with regard to investment and current cost.

— *Assistance:* School-run enterprises are a suitable place for providing vocational orientation on skilled occupations and on opportunities for continuing technical and vocational education for schools in the neighbourhood; in this connection, the school-run enterprise assists students in the introduction to the world of work.

— *Campaigning :*The above-mentioned tasks include the possibility of campaigning for skilled occupations in the region with the necessary information on training conditions (structure and duration of training, examinations, continuing education, boarding schools, costs, etc.)

— *Counselling:* The modern equipment of the school, the level of training of its teaching staff, the technical and information resources (technical library, collection of standards, learning media) allow the school to provide competent counselling to enterprises in terms of management (establishment of new enterprises, accounting, bookkeeping, etc.) and in technical terms (tool grinding, introduction to new technologies, etc.).

— *Innovation:* Since school-run enterprises are not immediately exposed to market pressures, they are suitable institutions for innovations of technical products and processes whose development can at the same time further vocational education of students, the continuing education of teaching staff and the cooperation with enterprises (technology transfer).

— *Promotion :* Students who are highly motivated and particularly efficient can be enabled by their school to acquire qualifications and take vocational and general examinations which allow them to go on to further education institutions; in this way, a special occupational elite is created in the medium term.

— *Learning:* Technical and vocational education, if organized appropriately, combines the technical and economic functions of the school-run enterprise, which offers students a unique opportunity during training to assimilate both thought and behaviour patterns of an enterprise.

— *Teaching staff* :In view of the teaching staff's dual function of having to produce for the market while at the same time making possible meaningful vocational education, the special requirements of this teaching model can be met only if there is teaching staff with different skills at a high technical, economic and didactic level as well as long practical experience and imagination in the way they teach (this is needed above all for the school head). As a rule, this ambitious model makes it necessary to recruit teaching staff with very different backgrounds, and special attention must in addition be given to the recruitment of staff for the acquisition of orders, for marketing and for sales.

A critique of instruction in school-run enterprises from the point of view of technical and vocational education theory

— *Place of learning :* School-run enterprises as a didactic system have so far been formed only in countries where enterprises do not take an active part in vocational education; where school-run enterprises have been formed, this has been done under the following conditions:

Tradition: An indispensable prerequisite for enterprises to play a major role in vocational education is a tradition-based attitude on the part of entrepreneurs and trade unions, which implies that they wish this and support it actively (as is the case in the Federal Republic of Germany); if this prerequisite is not fulfilled, technical schools, training centres and school-run enterprises are established as institutional and didactic variants of in-company training.

Elites: Countries who intend to industrialize their economy establish training institutions with a high general and technical standard, while making recruitment of trainees conditional upon the fulfilment of stringent admission requirements; the purpose is to train a technical elite for management positions in enterprises with a view to advancing the technical and industrial development of their country.

Cost reduction: on account of the considerable investment and running costs of school-run enterprise, an attempt is made to reduce operating costs and raise funds for further investments by means of production for the market.

Competence: the close connection between production and vocational education holds a major chance of avoiding the weaknesses of simulative didactic systems, thus making possible reality-based learning.

— *Organization of learning* :The establishment of school-run enterprises is usually the result of a prevailing deficit; this didactic system is intended to replace real-work learning in the company. In this connection, the following critical questions arise:

— The economic and financial situation of many schools requires that priority be given to production goals; but the recruitment of instructors from enterprises and the resulting socialization problems concerning patterns of thinking and behaviour can also bring about a situation in which such a school is dominated by economic considerations; another factor is the pressure exerted by the partner enterprises in order to achieve specific market goals with the help of the school.

— The learning climate in a school, the prevalence of curricula and examinations, and the socialization of teaching staff (recruited from higher education institutions) can bring about a situation in which learning · dominates while production is neglected.

These two contrary positions (and observable developments) of school-run enterprises when being faced with having to make a choice between 'real' and 'simulative' learning can be made congruent with the help of the following formula:

— A manufacturing company produces the quantity that can be sold on the market.

— A school-run enterprise produces the quantity that is required for teaching and practising, in other words, production for the market is used as a "vehicle" to reach the complete set of learning goals.

— *Teaching staff* :School-run enterprises depend for their functioning on teaching staff with high technical, economic, educational and innovatory competences plus an extraordinary commitment to the "pioneering phase" and stamina in the political and economic "tug-of-war" between the learning requirements made by the school and the enterprise's economic interest. This almost intractable problem has frequently led teaching staff to submit exclusively either to the interest of the company or to the requirements of learning.

Yet, it is this ambiguous position of the school-run enterprise, namely that it is not quite a school and not quite a company, which provides this didactic system with an educational openness, liveliness and innovative tendency that cannot be achieved by any other model.

Vocational competence can be imparted by way of different teaching models; but the extent to which the technical and vocational qualifications imparted are appropriate, flexible and transferable in modern industrial production and services and, in particular, the degree of autonomy in the workplace resulting from the ability for independent occupational problem solving, are decided by the model or combination of models chosen.

The Concept of Modules of Employable Skills (MES) Training

A continuous but regulated supply of different types and levels of well-trained and skilled human resources is one of the essential prerequisites to economic and industrial development. It has long been recognized by industry, crafts and commerce that vocational training is in itself an investment, as the quality and standard of goods produced and of services rendered depend to a large extent on the level and degree of skills that the staff involved possess. Many of the vocational training programmes that have been and are being used by technical assistance programmes in developing countries originated in the industrialized countries. They were often developed at times when changes in terms of new technologies, production processes, tools, equipment, materials, as well as in occupational profiles, occurred at far slower rates than in the period of rapid change which characterizes today's world. These training programmes were designed to meet the certification requirements of recognized national occupational profiles, as well as to suit the educational level of the locally available training population. The methodologies and instructional materials used for such programmes require technically and pedagogically well-trained and experienced staff. Because of the rigid, time-based structure of both the training programmes and the instructional materials, modifying them to changed or different training needs is in most cases difficult and time-consuming. The recognition that a new generation of flexible training concepts and programmes, on a modular basis, would be required to enable training authorities and industries to cope effectively and efficiently with fast-changing training needs, in many countries led to research and development work in this area.

In the early 1970s, the International Labour Organization (ILO) started its own research to develop a flexible, employment-oriented vocational training concept, as well as new types of instructional material, suitable for learner-based and instructor-led application. Studying and taking into consideration, where applicable, the results of similar developments from other sources, the ILO has over the past five years developed a modular vocational training approach using Modules of Employable Skills (MES). This approach follows present trends whereby the structures and contents of vocational training programmes are based on the competencies required to perform the tasks contained in a given job and/or national training specifications. MES developments have so far concentrated on the following areas:

— the concept itself in terms of procedures, forms, and other documents to carry out job, task and skill analysis, to develop, implement, control, monitor and evaluate vocational training programmes and to develop instructional materials;

— a bank of instructional materials in the form of learning elements;

— a concept, programmes and instructional materials for vocational training staff development.

Logical and acceptable divisions of work, in the form of technical tasks, are the basis for the development of MES training programmes. Global occupational profiles or technical fields of work, which are broken down into such tasks, can be used as initial task lists to support local programmes in line with national or specific occupational profiles. Banks of learning elements or of other suitable instructional materials can support the development of training programmes for these national and specific occupational profiles.

Social and economic developments often lead to the creation of new jobs comprising tasks from different occupational areas for which new training programmes have to be developed. Banks of task analysis data and of learning elements could facilitate the development of training programmes for such new jobs.

As the definition of a task is often subject to varying interpretations which might range, for example, from marking out an installation layout to the complete installation of an electric system in a building, it was decided to introduce a new term called the Modular Unit (MU), with a precise and clear definition which says that "a modular unit is a logical and acceptable division of work within a particular job, occupation or field of work with a clear start and finish and which would not normally be further subdivided." Where technology is of a standardized nature, the substantive content of a modular unit can be used on a global basis taken from the initial task list.

The modular units performed within given jobs are grouped into modules of employable skills. An MES job specification consists of a job description and a list and precise descriptions of those modular units performed within a given job.

Examples of employable skills show that in situations where only one craftsman is working, he/she will have to perform all those modular units required to complete a given job, in order to be usefully employable or self-employable. In situations where there is enough work to justify the employment of two or three workers, the module of employable skills of each worker would consist of clusters of related and often interlinked modular units, reflecting the division of work among them. In some employment situations, this can lead to very narrow specializations whereby a module of employable skill might consist of only one modular unit.

MES training programmes can be updated or expanded to suit new requirements. This is of particular importance when workers have to be updated to enable them to apply new technologies or work processes in their jobs, or when redundant workers need to be retrained for new employment opportunities. For example, the training programme for a simple electrician, who initially had to perform only ten modular units in his job, can be expanded to include training for nine more modular units required to carry out two newly introduced installation methods, and to connect three additional electric circuits.

The instructional material for use with MES training programmes was initially designed in the form of learning elements. These are self-contained instructional booklets, each covering a specific item of skill or knowledge. Each learning element consists of precisely formulated learning objectives:

— a list of required equipment, materials and aids;

— a list of other, related learning elements;

— instructional pages which contain short, concise texts and which are profusely illustrated;

— a progress check which is matched to the learning objectives of the element.

Learning elements of this type are suitable for both learner-based and instructor-based application. They contain, in the form of texts and illustrations, what a good instructor would explain and demonstrate to his trainees. Because of the short, concise texts and the many simple line illustrations, learning elements are readily adaptable to computer-based training, interactive training, or various distance learning techniques.

The concept of learning elements has been designed not only for MES training but also for use with other vocational training approaches. On the other hand, learning elements are not the only form of instructional material used for MES training. Other suitable instructional material from all kinds of sources can, and should be used whenever learning elements are not available or not applicable. To facilitate the proper selection of such material and the planning of lessons or instructional units (the term used for a lesson plan in MES training), a simple form has been developed for use by instructors. Well-prepared instructional units can also form the basis for learning elements to be developed at later dates. Learning elements are developed under the following six main categories:

— Work Safety (general and overriding while specific aspects of work safety are included in each element);

— Activities;

— Theory;

— Graphic Information/Circuitry;

— Technical Information, Materials/Components/ Methods;

— Technical Information, Tools/Equipment/Machines.

Learning elements from these categories can be compiled to form limited or comprehensive training programmes. Depending on the level of decision-making required for a worker to perform a given modular unit, activity learning elements can be supported by different types of information learning elements.

Learning elements which have initially been developed for training in a particular occupational area can, in many cases, also be used for training in other occupational areas. In-depth skills analysis is used to identify the learning elements and/or instructional units required to train a person to perform the steps of work of a given modular unit. Once correctly prepared, this document can be used as reference to facilitate the development of MES training programmes in many other training situations.

Learning elements or instructional units of a common and basic nature apply to many different modular units. Repetitive statements of their titles may therefore occur if a training programme has to be prepared for more than one modular unit.

There are arrangements of phase tests and the final performance test for a training programme. Accreditation and certification can be documented by introducing a skills passport with national or even regional validity.

The MES training cycle is applicable to initial training, upgrading, updating or retraining. One of the most important aspects of MES training is the systematic training of vocational training staff, in line with their job requirements, to plan, develop, implement, monitor and evaluate training programmes, and to develop the instructional material required for such programmes. Up to now, learning elements and related programme outlines have been developed to train staff in the above-mentioned aspects of MES training.

Appendix

Revised Recommendation Concerning Technical and Vocational Education

Preamble

The General Conference of the United Nations Educational, Scientific and Cultural Organisation, meeting in Paris at its eighteenth session, held from 17 October to 23 November 1974,

Recalling the constitutional responsibilities of the Organisation for the promotion of education,

Recognizing that technical and vocational education have to contribute to the maintenance of peace and friendly understanding between the various nations,

Considering that education must now be seen as a lifelong process,

Recognizing that technical and vocational education is a prerequisite for sustaining the complex structure of modern civilization and economic and social development,

Recalling the principles set forth in Articles 23 and 26 of the Universal Declaration of Human Rights guaranteeing all the right to work and to education, Considering therefore that all have a right to an education enabling full participation in contemporary society,

Taking into account the diversity of education systems throughout the world, as well as the particular and urgent needs of developing countries,

Considering that in spite of this diversity similar goals are pursued and similar questions and problems arise in all countries concerning technical and vocational education and that therefore common standards and measures are called for,

Having adopted for this purpose at its twelfth session the Recommendation concerning Technical and Vocational Education,

Recognizing however that the rapid technological and educational changes of the last decade require new, creative, and efficient efforts in technical and vocational education to improve education as a whole for social, economic and cultural development,

Having decided at its seventeenth session that in view of those changes this Recommendation should be revised in order to better serve Member States,

Noting that the International Labour Conference has adopted, over the years, a number of instruments dealing with various aspects of vocational guidance and vocational training and, in particular, the Vocational Guidance Recommendation, 1949, the Vocational Training (Agriculture) Recommendation, 1956, and the Vocational Training Recommendation, 1962, and that the

Conference, at its 59th session, had adopted substantive conclusions with a view to adoption, in 1975, of a new instrument or instruments on vocational guidance and vocational training,

Noting further the close collaboration between UNESCO and the International Labour Organisation (ILO) in drawing up their respective instruments so that they pursue harmonious objectives, avoiding duplication and conflict, and with a view to continued collaboration for effective implementation of the two instruments,

Adopts this Recommendation this nineteenth day of November 1974.

The General Conference recommends that when developing and improving technical and vocational education, Member States should apply the following provisions by taking whatever legislative or other steps may be required to give effect, within their respective territories, to the principles set forth in this Recommendation,

The General Conference recommends that Member States should bring this Recommendation to the knowledge of the authorities and bodies concerned with technical and vocational education,

The General Conference recommends that Member States should report to it, at such times and in such manner as shall be determined by it, on the action they have taken to give effect to the Recommendation.

Scope

1. This Recommendation applies to all forms and aspects of education which are technical and

vocational in nature provided either in educational institutions or under their authority, directly by public authorities, or through other forms of organized education, public or private.

2. For the purposes of this Recommendation: 'technical and vocational education' is used as a comprehensive term referring to those aspects of the educational process involving, in addition to general education, the study of technologies and related sciences and the acquisition of practical skills, attitudes, understanding and knowledge relating to occupations in various sectors of economic and social life. Technical and vocational education is further understood to be:

   a) an integral part of general education;

   b) a means of preparing for an occupational field;

   c) an aspect of continuing education.

3. Technical and vocational education, being part of the total educational process, is included in the term education as defined in the Convention and Recommendation against Discrimination in Education adopted by the General Conference of the United Nations Educational, Scientific and Cultural Organization at its eleventh session and the provisions of that Convention and Recommendation are therefore applicable to it.

4. This recommendation should be understood as setting forth general principles, goals and guidelines to be applied by each individual country according to needs and resources. The application of the provisions in their particulars and the timing of the implementation will therefore depend upon the conditions existing in a given country.

Technical and vocational education in relation to the educational process: objectives

5. Given immense scientific and technological development, either in progress or envisaged, which characterizes the present era, technical and vocational education should be a vital aspect of the educational process and in particular should:

   a) contribute to the achievement of society's goals of greater democratization and social, cultural and economic development, while at the same time developing the potential of individuals for active participation in the establishment and implementation of these goals;

   b) lead to an understanding of the scientific and technological aspects of contemporary civilization in such a way that men comprehend their environment and are capable of acting upon it while taking a critical view of the social, political and environmental implications of scientific and technological change.

6. Given the necessity for new relationships between education, working life, and the community as a whole, technical and vocational education should exist as part of a system of lifelong education adapted to the needs of each particular country. This system should be directed to:

   a) abolishing barriers between levels and areas of education, between education and employment, and between school and society through:

      i) the integration of technical and vocational and general education in all educational streams above primary level;

ii) the creation of open and flexible educational structures;

iii) the taking into account of individuals' educational needs and of the evolution of occupations and jobs;

b) improving the quality of life by permitting the individual to expand his intellectual horizons and to acquire and to constantly improve professional skills and knowledge while allowing society to utilize the fruits of economic and technological change for the general welfare.

7. Technical and vocational education should begin with a broad basic vocational education, thus facilitating horizontal and vertical articulation within the education system and between school and employment thus contributing to the elimination of all forms of discrimination and should be designed so that it:

a) is an integral part of everyone's basic general education in the form of initiation to technology and to the world of work;

b) may be freely and positively chosen as the means by which one develops talents, interests and skills leading to an occupation in the sectors listed in paragraph 2 or to further education;

c) allows access to other aspects and areas of education at all levels by being grounded on a solid general education and, as a result of the integration mentioned in paragraph 6(a), containing a general education component through all stages of specialization;

d) allows transfers from one field to another within technical and vocational education;

e) is readily available to all and for all appropriate types of specialization, within and outside formal education systems, and in conjunction or in parallel with training in order to permit educational, career and job mobility at a minimum age at which the general basic education is considered to have been acquired, according to the education system in force in each country;

f) is available on the above terms and on a basis of equality to women as well as men;

g) is available to disadvantaged and handicapped persons in special forms adapted to their needs in order to integrate them more easily into society.

8. In terms of the needs and aspirations of individuals, technical and vocational education should:

a) permit the harmonious development of personality and character and foster the spiritual and human values, the capacity for understanding, judgement, critical thinking and self-expression; .

b) prepare the individual to learn continuously by developing the necessary mental tools, practical skills and attitudes;

c) develop capacities for decision-making and the qualities necessary for active and intelligent participation, teamwork and leadership at work and in the community as a whole.

Policy, planning and administration

9. Policy should be formulated and technical and vocational education administered in support of the general objectives adopted for the educational process as well as for national and, if possible, regional social and economic requirements, and an appropriate legislative and financial framework adopted. Policy should be directed to both the structural and the qualitative improvement of technical and vocational education.

10. Particular attention should be given to planning the development and expansion of technical and vocational education:

    a) high priority should be placed on technical and vocational education in national development plans as well as in plans for educational reform;

    b) planning should be based upon a thorough evaluation of both short-term and long-term needs taking into consideration any variation in needs which may exist within a country;

    c) adequate provision for proper current and future allocation of financial resources should be a major element of planning;

    d) planning should be done by a responsible body or bodies having authority on the national level. This body should have available to it data which have been collated, analysed, synthesized and interpreted by qualified staff provided with adequate research facilities.

11. Planning should be responsible to national and, if possible, regional, economic and social trends, to

projected changes in demand for different classes by goods and services, and for different types of skills and knowledge in such a way that technical and vocational education may easily adapt to the evolving situation be it rural or urban. This planning should also be coordinated with current and projected training action and the evolution of employment.

12. While the education authorities should have primary responsibility, the following groups and authorities should be actively associated in policy formulation, and in the planning process. Structures, on both national and local levels, taking the form of public agencies or consultative or advisory bodies, should be created to permit this:

a) public authorities responsible for planning economic and social policy, labour and employment, and for the various occupational sectors (industry, agriculture, commerce);

b) representatives of non-governmental organizations within each occupation sector from among employers and workers;

c) any authority or body, such as a training body or extension services, responsible for out-of-school education and training;

d) representatives of those responsible - both in public education and in State recognized private education - for executing educational policy including teachers, examining bodies and administrators;

e) parent, former pupil, student and youth organizations;

f) representatives from the community at large.

13. Policies for the structural improvement of technical and vocational education should be established within the framework of broad policies designed to imp lement the principle of lifelong education through the creation of open, flexible and complementary structures for education, training and educational and vocational guidance, regardless of whether these activities take place within the system of formal education or outside it. In this respect consideration should be given to the following:

    a) multipurpose secondary education offering diversified curricula including work-study programmes;

    b) open tertiary institutions recruiting from a variety of sources and offering programmes ranging from short specialized ones to longer full-time programmes of integrated studies and professional specialization;

    c) establishing a system of equivalencies whereby credit is given for completion of any approved programme and recognition is granted educational and professional qualifications achieved through various means.

14. Policy should be directed to ensuring high quality in such a way as to exclude the possibility of any judgement which discriminates between the different educational streams, whatever their ultimate goal. In this respect special efforts should be made to ensure that technical and vocational education in rural areas meets the same standards as that offered in urban ones.

15. In order to ensure quality, responsible national authorities should establish certain criteria and standards, subject to periodic review and evaluation, applying in all aspects of technical and vocational education, including to the extent possible non-formal education for:

    a) all forms of recognition of achievement and consequent qualification;

    b) staff qualifications;

    c) ratios of teaching and training staff to learners;

    d) the quality of curricula and teaching materials;

    e) safety precautions for all learning environments;

    f) physical facilities, building, workshop layouts, quality and type of equipment.

16. Policies should be established fostering research related to technical and vocational education, with particular emphasis on its potential within lifelong education, and directed to its improvement. This research should be carried out by competent staff on national and institutional levels as well as through individual initiative. To this end:

    a) special emphasis should be placed on curriculum development, research concerning teaching and learning methods and materials, and where the need exists, on technologies and techniques applied to development problems;

    b) financial resources and physical facilities should be made available through institutions of higher education, specialized research institutions and professional organizations for applying the results of this research on an experimental basis in representatively selected institutions for technical and vocational education;

c) channels should be created for the widespread dissemination and rapid application of the positive results of research and experimentation;

d) the effectiveness of technical and vocational education should be evaluated using, among other data, relevant statistics including those concerning part-time enrolments and dropout rates which are in some cases neglected;

e) particular attention should be given to all research efforts to humanize working conditions.

17. Provision should be made within administrative structures for evaluation, supervisory and accreditation services, staffed by technical and vocational education specialists, to ensure the rapid application of new research findings and to maintain standards:

   a) evaluation services as a whole should ensure the quality and smooth operation of technical and vocational education by continuous review and action directed to constant improvement of staff, facilities and programmes;

   b) supervisory services for the staff should encourage improvement in the quality of teaching by providing guidance and advice and recommending continuing education;

   c) all programmes of technical and vocational education, in particular those offered by private bodies, should be subject to approval by the public authorities through some means of accreditation or form of public inspection.

18. Particular attention should be given to the material resources required for technical and vocational education. Priorities should be carefully established with due regard for immediate needs and the probable directions of future expansion and adequate cost controls introduced:

    a) institutional planning should be directed to ensuring maximum efficiency and flexibility in use;

    b) the planning, construction and equipping of facilities should be carried out in collaboration with specialist teachers and educational architects and with due regard for their purpose, prevailing local factors and relevant research;

    c) adequate funds should be allocated for recurrent expenditure for supplies and maintenance and repair of equipment.

Technical and vocational aspects of general education

19. An initiation to technology and to the world of work should be an essential component of general education without which this education is incomplete. An understanding of the technological facet of modern culture in both its positive and negative attributes, and an appreciation of work requiring practical skills should thereby be acquired. This initiation should further be a major concern in educational reform and change with a view to greater democratization of education. It should be a required

element in the curriculum, beginning in primary education and continuing through the early years of secondary education.

20. Opportunities for general technical and vocational initiation should continue to be available to those who wish to avail themselves of it within the educational system and outside it in places of work or community centres.

21. The technical and vocational initiation in the general education of youth should fulfil the educational requirements of all ranges of interest and ability. It should mainly perform three functions:

    a) to enlarge educational horizons by serving as an introduction to the world of work and the world of technology and its products through the exploration of materials, tools, techniques and the process of production, distribution and management as a whole, and to broaden the learning process through practical experience;

    b) to orient those with the interest and ability towards technical and vocational education as preparation for an occupational field or towards training outside the formal education system;

    c) to promote in those who will leave formal education at whatever level but with no specific occupational aims or skills, attitudes of mind and ways of thought likely to enhance their aptitudes and potential, to facilitate the choice of an occupation and access to a first job, and to permit them to continue their vocational training and personal education.

22. Required general technical and vocational studies in the schools having great importance for the orientation and education of youth programmes, should include a proper balance between theoretical and practical work. A properly structured programme of such studies should be drawn up by the competent authorities in collaboration with the professional community and with those responsible for technical and vocational education. These programmes should:

   a) be based upon a problem-solving and experimental approach and involve experience in planning methods and decision-making;

   b) introduce the learner to a broad spectrum of technological fields and at the same time to productive work situations;

   c) develop a certain command of valuable practical skills such as tool use, repair and maintenance and safety procedures, whether applicable to future education, training and employment or to leisure time, and a respect for their value;

   d) develop an appreciation of good design and craftsmanship and the ability to select goods on the basis of their quality;

   e) develop the ability to communicate including the use of graphical means;

   f) develop the ability to measure and calculate accurately;

   g) be closely related to the local environment without, however, being limited to it.

23. The technical and vocational initiation in programmes of general educational enrichment for older youth and adults should be directed to enabling those engaged in working life to:

    a) understand the general implications of technical change, its impact on their professional and private lives, and how man may shape this change;

    b) to use practical skills for improving the home and community environment and thus the quality of life and, in appropriate conditions, for productive leisure-time activities.

Technical and vocational education as preparation for an occupational field

24. Given disparities that may exist between formal education, whether secondary or tertiary, and the employment and career opportunities available, the highest priority should be given to technical and vocational education which prepares young people to exercise occupations in the sectors covered by this recommendation. Consequently the structure and content of traditional education, whether general or technical and vocational, should be adapted accordingly through:

    a) the diversification of secondary education in the later stages so that it may be pursued in conjunction with employment or training, or may lead to employment or to higher education, thereby offering to all youth educational options corresponding to their needs;

b) the introduction of new programmes into tertiary education more relevant to the career needs of young adults;

c) the development of educational structures and programmes on all levels centred on organized and flexible interchange between educational institutions including training institutions and those responsible for employment in the various occupational sectors.

25. Technical and vocational education as preparation for an occupational field should provide the foundation for productive and satisfying careers and should:

a) lead to the acquisition of broad knowledge and basic skills applicable to a number of occupations within a given field so that the individual is not limited by his education in his freedom of occupational choice, and later transfer from one field to another in the course of working life is facilitated;

b) at the same time offer a thorough and specialized preparation for initial employment and effective training within employment;

c) provide the background in terms of skills, knowledge and attitudes, for continuing education at any point in the individual's working life.

26. Premature and narrow specialization should be avoided:

a) in principle 15 should be considered the lower age limit for beginning specialization;

b) a period of common studies concerning basic knowledge and skills should be required for each broad occupational sector before a special branch is chosen.

27. Because it is desirable that women seek wider participation in all kinds of occupations outside family and domestic activities, they should have the same educational opportunities available to them as men in order to prepare for an occupation and should be encouraged to take advantage of these through appropriate legislative measures and widespread distribution of information concerning these opportunities.

28. Special provision should be made for out-of-school and unemployed youth and children of migrant workers with the minimum or less of primary education, as well as for those not entering education or training programmes after completion of compulsory schooling, in order that they may acquire employable skills.

29. Given the necessity of integrating the physically and mentally disadvantaged into society and its occupations, the same educational opportunities should be available to them as to the non-handicapped in order that they may achieve qualification for an occupation; special measures or special institutions may be required.

Organization

30. Technical and vocational education as preparation for an occupational field should be organized on a national or, if possible, regional basis, so as to respond positively to overall social, economic and

educational requirements and to the needs of different groups of the population without discrimination.

31. Several organizational patterns of technical and vocational education, including both full-time and part-time options should exist within each country. The following patterns of organization for example should be considered:

a) full-time including practical training as well as general education, provided in an educational establishment, either comprehensive or specialized;

b) part-time programmes such as the following in which general education and theoretical and broad practical aspects of the occupational field are given in an educational establishment while specialized practical training is acquired during work in the chosen occupation:

i) the day-release system providing for young workers and apprentices to attend an educational establishment at least one day a week and preferably two;

ii) the sandwich system under which periods in an educational institution alternate with training periods in a factory, farm, business establishment or other undertaking;

iii) the block-release system whereby young workers are released to attend courses for one or two short periods of at least ten to fifteen weeks in total length per year which may be especially adapted to conditions in areas of low population density by provision of boarding facilities.

32. The responsible authorities should encourage part-time education, therefore:

    a) these programmes should be available directly after completion of minimum compulsory or required schooling, and should continue to be available to the highest level of formal education;

    b) the educational qualifications acquired by this means should be equivalent to those acquired by full-time education;

    c) where employers are responsible for the practical training aspect for part-time students, this training should be as broad as possible serving the educational and training needs of the individual, and should meet national standards.

33. In view of the increasing requirement for highly qualified middle-level manpower in all fields, and the increasing numbers completing secondary education or its equivalent, the development of programmes of technical and vocational education corresponding to further qualifying tertiary education should be given high priority. The following patterns of organization should be considered:

    a) period of from one to two years of guided work experience followed by a part-time or briefer full-time programmes of specialization;

    b) part-time programmes;

    c) full-time programmes as an extension of programmes given in specialized secondary institutions or given in tertiary institutions.

34. The high cost of equipment for the practical component of technical and vocational education

requires that this be organized so that benefits received are in proportion to the cost. Consideration should be given to the following as a means of achieving this:

a) centralized workshops, or mobile units, could be used to serve several educational institutions;

b) workshops attached to educational institutions could be designed so that they are suitable for use by the community at large particularly for continuing education programmes;

c) although workshops and laboratories in advanced secondary or tertiary institutions should be designed primarily for pedagogical purposes, they might also be equipped and staffed so that equipment for use in technical and vocational studies in general education may be produced.

35. Enterprises should be closely associated in the practical training of those preparing for occupations in their particular sector, and should be encouraged to take responsibility, in co-operation with educational institutions, for the organization of this training.

Programme content

36. All programmes of technical and vocational education as preparation for an occupational field should:

a) aim at providing scientific knowledge, technical versatility and the broad skills and knowledge required for rapid adaptation to new ideas and procedures and for steady career development;

b) be based on an analysis of broad occupational requirements worked out for the long term between education authorities including organizations representing educational research and administration and employment authorities and occupational organizations concerned;

c) include a proper balance between general subjects, science and technology, and studies of both the theoretical and practical aspects of the occupational field, with the practical component in all cases related to the theoretical one;

d) stress developing a sense of professional values and responsibilities from the standpoint of human needs.

37. In particular programmes should:

a) whenever possible be interdisciplinary in character as many occupations now require knowledge and training in two or more traditional areas of study;

b) be based on curricula designed around core knowledge and skills;

c) include studies of the social and economic aspects of the occupational field as a whole;

d) include the study of at least one foreign language of international use which, while conducive to a higher cultural level, will give special emphasis to the requirements of communication and the acquisition of a scientific and technical vocabulary;

e) include an introduction to organizational and planning skills;

f) emphasize instruction in safety procedures relative to the materials and equipment used in a given occupational field and the importance of safe working conditions and the health aspects relative to the occupation as a whole.

38. While based on the above general principles and components, and thus pursuing in all cases broader educational aims, programmes in their practical aspect should be designed taking into account special occupational requirements with regard to the particular executive, organizational, analytical and practical skills required.

39. Technical and vocational education programmes leading to university qualification, while encouraging research and offering high-level specialization, should be developed with particular attention to:

   (a) the inclusion of components directed to developing attitudes whereby those with broad responsibilities in technological fields constantly relate their professional tasks to larger human goals;

   (b) relating more closely higher technical and vocational education for the industrial and agricultural sectors to the requirements of these sectors. In this regard consideration should be given to creating within tertiary institutions, centres for the testing and certification of industrial and agricultural products, supervised by the public authorities and serving both educational and research purposes.

40. Programmes of technical and vocational education as preparation for occupations within the agricultural sector should be designed in accordance with the overall social and economic requirements of rural development. Therefore:

a) both general aspects and the technical and vocational aspects, while adapted in terms of both organization and content to the special requirements of agricultural occupations, should be of the same quality as those for other occupational areas;

b) programmes should be directed to the development and application of technologies especially suited to rural development through close co-ordination between education and extension services and between these and research services and institutions;

c) programmes should be directed to preparing qualified people for all types of occupations and ranges of technical competence necessary for rural development;

d) programmes should be broadly conceived, including in addition to the special occupational area, an introduction to the commercial aspects of agriculture and the functioning of rural economic institutions.

41. Where lack of resources limits the expansion of technical and vocational education, emphasis in the initial stages should be placed on developing programmes for occupations in areas of critical manpower shortage, and in areas of immediate development potential.

42. Programmes preparing for occupations in small industry, individual farming or the artisan trades, whether urban or rural, and particularly for self-employment, should include commercial studies enabling those engaged in such occupations to take

responsibility not only for production, but also for marketing, competent management and the rational organization of the whole enterprise.

43. Programmes leading to occupations in the business and commercial sector should include:

a) thorough grounding in the methods and skills developed as a result of the application of technology to business and office management and particularly to the acquisition and processing of information;

b) training in the organizational and management skills required for the smooth operation of enterprises in all economic sectors;

c) an introduction to marketing and distribution procedures.

44. Special attention should be given to developing programmes for preparing personnel at all levels for the social services sector (e.g. community and family work, nursing and paramedical occupations, nutrition and food technology, home economics and environmental improvement). Those programmes should:

a) emphasize the relation of the special occupational field to raising standards of living in terms of food, clothing, housing, medical services, the quality of family life or that of the environment as the case may be;

b) be well adapted to the special requirements of local conditions in particular those of climate and geography, materials available and community organization and social patterns.

Technical and vocational education as continuing education

45. The development and expansion of technical and vocational education as continuing education, both within and outside the formal education system, and within the framework of lifelong education, should be a priority objective of all educational strategies and broad provision should be made for allowing everyone, whatever the educational qualifications achieved prior to employment, to continue both their professional and general education.

46. In addition to permitting adults to make up deficiencies in general education or professional qualifications, which has often been the only objective of continuing education, it should now:

   a) offer possibilities of personal development and professional advancement;

   b) permit the updating and refreshing of knowledge and practical abilities and skills in the occupational field;

   c) enable the individual to adapt to technological changes in his occupation or to enter another occupation if these changes render his particular job obsolete;

   d) be available throughout working life without restriction of age, sex, prior education and training or position;

   e) be broad in scope, including general education elements, and not simply specialized training for one particular job.

47. The appropriate authorities should be encouraged to provide the basic conditions for technical and vocational education as continuing education, including consideration of measures providing for paid educational leave or other forms of financial aid.

48. The technical and vocational aspect of continuing education should actively be encouraged through such means as:

    a) widespread dissemination of information concerning the programmes available, and how one may take advantage of existing opportunities, including full use of mass media to this end;

    b) recognition of successful completion of programmes in terms of remuneration and professional advancement.

49. Those responsible for organizing programmes of continuing technical and vocational education recognized by the public authorities should consider the following forms:

    a) courses given during working hours at the place of work;

    b) fuller part-time courses especially designed for continuing education given in secondary and tertiary institutions, already staffed and equipped for technical and vocational education;

    c) evening and weekend courses given in the above types of institutions or in community centres;

    d) correspondence courses;

    e) courses given on educational television;

    f) periodic seminars;

g) inter-enterprise programmes;

h) informal discussion groups created and organized on the initiative of students.

50. The following forms of organization of leave should be considered:

a) day release;

b) block release of varying lengths;

c) release for one or more hours during the working day.

51. Programmes of technical and vocational education as continuing education should:

a) be designed and taught on the basis of the special requirements of adults, and use teaching methods which take into account the expertise which they have already acquired;

b) contain a built-in mechanism for rapid adjustment to the needs of particular individuals or groups and to technological change.

52. Special provision should be made for groups with particular requirements:

a) in the case of women, because of the necessity of periods of absence from the labour force imposed by maternity and family responsibilities, in order to enable them to update their knowledge and to improve their professional skills for re-entry into employment;

b) to enable older workers to adapt to new occupations;

c) to provide foreign workers and handicapped workers with specific facilities for pre-training to enable them to adapt to a training programme or to working life;

d) the resources of continuing education should be used to offer unskilled and semiskilled workers the opportunity to improve their qualifications.

53. Particular attention should be paid to the development of continuing education programmes suitable in rural areas in terms of content, physical location and time of year offered.

Guidance

54. Guidance should be viewed as a continuous process and a vital element in education, directed to aiding all to make positive educational and occupational choices. It should ensure that the individual be provided with the necessary prerequisites:

   a) to become aware of his interests and abilities and able to set himself precise objectives;

   b) to pursue a course of education, whether preparatory or continuing, commensurate with these;

   c) to make decisions concerning his occupation, both in the initial and later stages, which lead to a satisfying career;

   d) to facilitate transitions between education and employment at whatever level or stage.

55. Guidance services on the national, local and institutional levels should ensure that the paths are

kept open between education and initial training and employment, and employment and continuing education and training through:

a) close liaison and coordination with training, counselling, employment and placement services;

b) ensuring that all necessary information concerning employment and career opportunities is available and actively disseminated;

c) ensuring that those in employment have access to information concerning opportunities in continuing education and training.

56. While emphasizing the needs of the individual, guidance for young people should be accompanied by information which gives them a realistic view of the opportunities available in a given occupational cluster, including information regarding probable developments in the market and in employment structures, and what may be expected in terms of remuneration, career advancement and possibilities for occupational change.

57. Particular attention should be given to guidance for girls and women:

a) this guidance should cover the same broad range of education, training and employment opportunities as for boys and men;

b) it should systematically encourage girls and women to take advantage of the opportunities available to them.

58. Guidance given in the technical and vocational aspects of general education during the observation or orientation cycle of secondary schooling should:

a) cover a broad range of occupations with supplementary visits to work places and acquaint the student with the eventual necessity of choosing an occupation and the importance of this choice being as rational as possible;

b) aid students in making a positive choice concerning educational streams or options for those wishing to pursue technical and vocational education as preparation for an occupational field or training programmes outside the educational system, and aid those not continuing their formal education or entering training to find employment, while encouraging then to continue their education at a later date.

59. Guidance in technical and vocational education as preparation for an occupational field should:

a) inform the student of the various possibilities open in the particular field of interest, the educational background required and the possibilities for later continuing education available;

b) encourage the student to choose an educational programme which will limit his later employment options as little as possible;

c) follow the progress of the student during the educational programmes;

d) supplement the later stages of the programmes by short periods of work experience and study of real work situations.

60. Guidance in technical and vocational education as continuing education should:

a) help the employed adult choose the programme of continuing education most suited to his needs;

b) enable him to place himself in relation to the various levels of study and afford him the means of making effective choices.

61. Guidance should be given on the basis of:

a) knowledge of the individual which takes account of the social and family factors influencing his attitudes and expectations;

b) information obtained from objective evaluation of the results of testing including aptitude tests;

c) knowledge of his educational achievements and/or achievements in employment;

d) knowledge of employment and career opportunities as well as job satisfaction in the occupational sector in which he is interested or engaged and of demands made;

e) medical records indicating whether the student is physically able to pursue a given occupation.

62. The effectiveness of guidance services should continually be assessed and statistics kept on both the national and institutional levels through:

a) the keeping of cumulative records concerning the education of the students as well as follow-up records concerning his employment;

b) a built-in system of evaluation of both quality of staff performance and the methods used in order to effect change or improvement where needed.

The teaching and learning processes

63. In all aspects of technical and vocational education,

the methodology of learning should assume equal importance in the teaching and learning process with the subject-matter itself. All aspects of technical and vocational education should be oriented to the needs of the learner and directed to motivating him, and methods and materials developed accordingly.

64. Theory and practice should form an integrated whole: what is learned in the laboratory, workshop or in enterprises should be directly related to the mathematical and scientific foundations of the particular operation or process, and conversely, technical theory, as well as the mathematics and science sustaining it, should be illustrated through their practical applications.

65. Full use should be made of the resources provided by educational technology, with special emphasis on the methods and materials of self-education, in particular audiovisual aids, including multi-media systems, programmed instruction and the use of mass media.

66. The methods and materials used in technical and vocational education should be carefully adapted to the group to be taught. In this respect:

   a) where the language of instruction differs from the native language, teaching materials should make maximum use of numerical and graphical representation, written material being kept to a minimum;

   b) where materials developed in one country are adapted for use in another, this adaptation should be carefully made with due regard to local factors.

67. Machines and equipment used in workshops in educational institutions should be geared to the level

and training of the users. This equipment should be simple and designed especially for pedagogical purposes without however being obsolete or teaching obsolete procedures. Training using complex equipment may be given more appropriately and efficiently on the job.

Evaluation

68. Evaluation should be an integral part of the teaching and learning process in technical and vocational education, and its major function should be the development of the particular individual in accordance with his interests and capacities.

69. Although standards of performance should be upheld, evaluation of the student's work should be made on a total basis considering among others his class participation, his interest and attitude, his relative progress, allowance being made for his aptitudes, and examinations and other tests.

70. Students should participate in the evaluation of their own progress and the evaluation of student work should have a system of feedback built into it so that learning problems and their causes may be identified and steps taken to correct them.

71. Continuous evaluation of the teaching process should be made by both teachers and their supervisors, with the participation of students as well, in order to determine the effectiveness of the methods and materials used, and to devise alternatives should the need arise. Continuous evaluation of the teaching-learning process should be undertaken with the

participation of representatives from the occupational fields concerned.

Staff

72. To enhance the achievement of the objectives of technical and vocational education, a priority should be given to the recruitment and preparation of adequate numbers of well-qualified and competent teachers, administrators and guidance staff, and to the provision of the necessary training and other facilities to enable them to function effectively in their profession.

73. The emoluments and conditions of service which are offered should compare favourably with those enjoyed by persons with similar qualification and experience in other occupational sectors. In particular, promotions, salaries and pension scales for technical and vocational education staff should take into account any relevant experience acquired in employment outside the educational sector.

Teaching Staff

74. All teachers in technical and vocational education, including those who teach only practice, should be considered an integral part of the teaching profession and as such should be recognized as having the same status as their colleagues in other fields. In this regard:

    a) the Recommendation concerning the Status of Teachers adopted by the Special Intergovernmental

Conference on the Status of Teachers on 5 October 1966 is applicable to them especially as regards the provisions concerning preparation for a profession and continuing education; employment and career; the rights and responsibilities of teachers; conditions for effective teaching and learning; teachers' salaries; social security;

b) arbitrary distinctions between teachers employed by various types of educational institutions, e.g. specialized technical and vocational institutions and general education institutions, should be eliminated.

75. Teachers involved in any aspect of technical and vocational education, whether on a full-time or part-time basis, should posses the personal, ethical, professional and teaching qualities essential for the accomplishment of their work.

76. Teachers of technical and vocational aspects in general education should:

a) be familiar with a broad range of specialities;

b) develop the ability to relate these to each other as well as to the larger social, economic and historical and cultural context;

c) where this aspect of technical and vocational education serves primarily an occupation or educational orientation function, be able to give guidance.

77. Considering technical and vocational education as preparation for an occupational field, teachers in this area should have special qualifications depending on the occupation for which they are preparing students:

a) if the occupational field requires primarily practical skills, the teacher should himself have long employment experience in the exercise of these skills;

b) if students are to be prepared for technician or middle management positions, teachers should have a thorough knowledge, preferably acquired through appropriate practical experience, of the special requirements of this type of position;

c) if the occupational field requires research and theoretical analysis, e.g. an engineering field, the teacher should have a university education and be actively engaged in research himself.

78. Considering technical and vocational education as continuing education, teachers in this area should, in addition to the special preparation for teaching adults, have an adequate knowledge of the working environment of their students and have specialized knowledge and skills in their teaching field.

79. Skilled professionals employed in appropriate sectors outside education should be invited to teach, at suitable points in technical and vocational education, certain programmes in schools, universities or other educational institutions in order to link the world of work more closely to the classroom.

80. Teachers of general subjects in institutions which offer technical and vocational education, in addition to the usual qualification, both professional and in their teaching field, should receive a special initiation concerning the objectives and requirements of technical and vocational education.

81. Preparation for technical and vocational teaching should be given as a tertiary programme, thereby requiring completion of secondary education or its equivalent for entrance. All types of programme should be designed with the following objectives in mind:

    a) to maintain standards of education and professional preparation in vigour for the teaching profession as a whole and to contribute to the raising of these overall standards;

    b) to develop in the future teacher the ability to teach both the theoretical and practical aspects of his field;

    c) to ensure that the teacher will be qualified, with minimum further training, to teach other groups than those for which he was prepared initially.

82. Varied and flexible programmes, full-time and part-time, adapted to the special requirements of a wide variety of recruitment sources as well as to those of the field to be taught and the group or groups to be taught should be available.

83. In those cases where it is difficult for intending technical and vocational teachers to acquire employment experience, consideration should be given to creating units, attached to teacher-training institutions, for the production of equipment and teaching materials for the schools in which intending teaching staff would be required to work for varying lengths of time.

84. The professional preparation of all technical and vocational teachers should include the following elements:

a) educational theory both in general and as especially applying to technical and vocational education;

b) educational psychology and sociology as it especially applies to the group or groups for which the future teacher will be responsible;

c) special teaching methods appropriate to the field of technical and vocational education for which the future teacher is preparing and the groups to be taught, in methods of evaluation of student work, and in classroom management;

d) training in the choice and use of the whole range of modern teaching techniques and aids presupposing the use of up-to-date methods and materials in the programme of professional preparation itself;

e) training in how to create and produce appropriate teaching materials, of special importance in those cases where technical and vocational materials are in short supply;

f) a period of supervised practice teaching experience before appointment to a teaching post;

g) an introduction to educational and occupational guidance methods as well as to educational administration;

h) a thorough grounding in safety and emphasis on the ability to teach safe working practice and habitually to set a good working example.

85. Staff responsible for the preparation of technical and vocational teachers should have obtained the highest qualifications possible in their field:

a) teacher-educators responsible for special technical and vocational fields should have qualifications in their field equivalent to those of special subjects staff in other institutions and programmes of higher education, including advanced degrees and employment experience in related occupational fields;

b) teacher-educators responsible for the pedagogical aspect of teacher preparation should themselves be experienced teachers in technical and vocational education and should possess the highest qualifications in a specialized field of education.

86. Staff responsible for the preparation of technical and vocational teachers should be actively engaged in research in their field and provision should be made for this in terms of a reasonable teaching load and access to appropriate facilities.

87. Teaching staff should be encouraged to continue their education, whatever the field in which they specialize, and should have the necessary means to do so. This continuing education, which should be made available in a wide range of facilities, should include:

a) periodic review and updating of knowledge and skills in the special field;

b) periodic updating of professional skills and knowledge;

c) periodic work in the occupational sector relating to the special field.

88. Account should be taken of a teacher's achievements in continuing education when the responsible

authorities consider questions of promotion, seniority and status concerning him.

Administrative and guidance staff

89. Administrative responsibilities for technical and vocational education programmes should be entrusted to persons with the following qualifications:

   a) teaching experience in a field of technical and vocational education;

   b) proficiency acquired through study and employment experience in one of the fields taught in the programme;

   c) a broad vision of technical and vocational education as a whole and of the interrelation of the various aspects;

   d) a knowledge of administrative techniques.

90. The heads of establishments in technical and vocational education should receive adequate administrative assistance so that they can devote most of their time to the highly important educational and scientific aspects of their work. Technical and vocational education establishments should have sufficient staff to provide the following services:

   a) advice and guidance for candidates and students;

   b) the preparation, supervision and coordination of all practical work and experiments;

   c) the maintenance of instruments, apparatus and tools in workshops and laboratories.

91. Administrators should keep up to date with new administrative techniques and trends through programmes of continuing education. Prospective administrators should receive special training in methods and problems involved in the task. This preparation should include:

    a) management methods appropriate to educational administration;

    b) methods of allocation of available resources given the objectives of the various programmes for which they will be responsible;

    c) planning methods.

92. Guidance staff should receive special preparation for their tasks whether they are specialists or are teachers serving also as guidance staff. This preparation should be equipped to make objective assessments of aptitude, interest and motivation and to have at hand up-to-date information concerning career and education opportunities. During this preparation they should acquire a direct knowledge of the economy and the world of work through systematically organized visits to enterprises and periods of time spent in enterprises. Guidance staff should be required and provided with facilities - including the opportunity for practical experience - to keep up with new methods of guidance and information as to new or changed educational training and employment opportunities.

International co-operation

93. Member States should give priority to international

co-operation in the field of technical and vocational education.

a) This co-operation, whether in the framework of bilateral or multilateral agreements, or through international organizations, should be directed to improving the quality of technical and vocational education and developing and expanding it where necessary.

b) Every effort should be made to co-ordinate within any given country the international assistance activities in the field of technical and vocational education.

94. Member States should take special measures to provide foreigners (in particular migrants and refugees) and their children living within their territory with technical and vocational education. Such measures should take into account the special needs of such persons in the host country as well as in view of their possible return to their country.

95. Provision should be made at national, regional and international levels for the regular exchange of information, documentation, and materials of international interest obtained from research and development efforts on all levels concerning technical and vocational education, in particular:

a) publications concerning, among others, comparative education, psychological and pedagogical problems affecting general and technical and vocational education, and current trends;

b) information and documentation concerning curriculum development, methods and materials, study opportunities abroad, employment opportunities including manpower requirements, working conditions and social benefits;

c) teaching materials and social benefits;

d) mass media programmes of an informational or pedagogical character.

96. Regional co-operation among countries having a common cultural heritage and facing common problems in the development or extension of technical and vocational education should be highly encouraged through:

a) periodic meetings on the ministerial·level and the establishment of a standing committee or organization to review policies formulated and actions taken;

b) the creation of joint facilities for higher level research, the development of prototype materials and equipment, and the preparation of staff for the training of teachers where the costs of such facilities are too high to be sustained by any one country in a given region.

97. The development of both written and audiovisual teaching and learning materials which are suitable for international or regional use should be considered a priority area in international co-operation. These materials should contribute to ιhe progressive establishment of common standards for professional qualifications acquired through technical and vocational education.

98. Member States should encourage the creation of a climate of opinion favourable to international co-operation in the field of technical and vocational education through:

a) teacher and student fellowships and exchanges;

b) establishment of sustained contacts between similar institutions in different countries;

c) provision of employment experience abroad, particularly when opportunities at home are limited.

99. To facilitate international co-operation, Member States should apply within technical and vocational education internationally recommended standards and norms relating in particular to:

a) system of measure;

b) scientific and technical symbols;

c) occupational qualifications;

d) information processing;

e) equivalencies of qualifications acquired through technical and vocational education implying standardization of curricula and testing, including aptitude tests, for some technical fields;

f) safety and security through testing of materials and products.

100. Internationally recommended standards and norms concerning technical and vocational education should be continuously evaluated through sustained research concerning the effectiveness of their application in the various countries especially in order to facilitate the establishment of equivalence of qualifications and free movement of individuals between the different national systems of education.

Bibliography

Conger, Stuart, *Policies and Guidelines for Educational and Vocational Guidance*, UNESCO Paris, 1994.

Grubb, W. N., J. Kalman, M. Castellano, C. Brown, and D. Bradby, *'Readin', Writin', and 'Rithmetic One More Time: The Role of Remediation in Vocational Education and Job Training*, 1991.

Hegelheimer, A., *Financing of vocational training*, German Foundation for International Development (DSE), 1986.

Hollinshead, B., *Trends and Development of Technical and Vocational Education*, Unesco, 1990.

Hudis, P, D., Bradby, C. Brown, E. G. Hoachlander, K. Levesque, and S. Nachuck, *Meeting the Personnel Needs of the Health Care Industry Through Vocational Education Programs*, Berkeley, CA:National Center for Research in Vocational Education, 1992.

Little, J. W., *Two Worlds: Vocational and Academic Teachers in Comprehensive High Schools*, 1992.

Plihal, J., M.A. Johnson, C. Bentley, C. Morgaine, T. Liang, *Integration of Vocational and Academic Education: Theory and Practice*, 1992.

Ryan, P. (ed.), *International comparisons of vocational education and training for intermediate skills*, The Falmer Press, 1991.

UNESCO, *Vocational Guidance for Equal Access and Opportunity for Girls and Women in Technical and Vocational Education*, Paris, 1996.

UNESCO, The Integration of General and Technical and Vocational Education - Trends and Issues in *Technical and Vocational Education* 3, 1986.

UNESCO and International Labour Organisation, *Technical and Vocational Education and Training*, Paris/Geneva, 1964.

UNESCO, "A Framework for Improvement of Educational and Vocational Guidance Services for Girls and Women in Asia and the Pacific", *Bangkok, UNESCO Principal Regional Office for Asia and the Pacific*, 1987.

UNESCO, "Convention on technical and vocational education", *adopted by the General Conference at its twenty-fifth session,* 10 November, Paris, 1989.

World Bank, "Vocational and technical education and training", *A World Bank Policy Paper*, Washington, D.C.: World Bank, 1991.

Index

Australian National Training Authority (ANTA), 57

Basic Education for Skills Training (BEST), 84

Colleges of Advanced Education (CAEs), 58
Combined to establish Group Training Units (CGTU), 67
Curriculum and Examinations Board (CEB), 138

Darwinian framework, 31
Department of Non-formal Education (DNFE), 92
Department of Skill Department (DSD), 92
Department of Vocational Education (DOVE), 91
Didactic micromodels, 203
Digital photographs, 187
Distance education, 5

Economic progress, hallmark of, 33
Educational Guidance, 126
Educational technology, 6
Employment-related competency formation, 34

General Certificate of Education (GCE), 82
Global consumer market, 4

Health-related problems, 3
Human Resources Development Fund (HRDF), 71

Indira Ghandi National Open University (IGNOU), 46
Informal social processes, 204
Information and Communication Technologies (ICTs), 11
Information Technology (IT), 4
Institute of Guidance Counsellors (IGC), 124
Institute of Technical Education (ITE), 83
International Labour Organization (ILO), 227
Intra-trade practice, 33

King Mongkut's Institute of Technology (KMIT), 93
Knowledge revolution, 36

Laissez-faire approach, 27
Learner-friendly approach, 186

Learning environments, 183
Leaving Certificate Vocational Programme (LCVP), 145
Life support system, 3
Life-long guidance, 135

Modular Unit (MU), 228
Modules of Employable Skills (MES), 226
Multi-channel distance learning, 30

Nanyang Technological University (NTU), 87
National Council for Curriculum and Assessment (NCCA), 138
National University of Singapore (NUS), 87

Occupational destination, 34
Open and Distance Learning (ODL), 5
Open learning programmes, 178

Penilaian Menengah Rendah (PMR), 69
Private Higher Educational Institutions (PHEIs), 71

Quasi-school systems, 209

Recognition of Current Competence (RCC), 193
Recognition of the Prior Learning (RPL), 35

School curriculum, 7
Sijil Tinggi Pereskolahan Malaysia (SPTM), 70
Singapore Hotel Association Training and Education Centre (SHATEC), 85
Skill utilization, 204
Student administrative systems, 180
Sustainable agriculture, 3
Sustainable development, 3
Systematic learning processes, 211

Technical and Further Education (TAFE), 56
Technical and Vocational Education (TVE), 46
Technical and Vocational Education and Training (TVET), 2
Technical Education and Skills Development Authority (TESDA), 77
Technological University of the Philippines (TUP), 79

Urban civilisation, 2
Urbanisation, 2

Vocational Education and Training (VET), 56
Vocational Education Program (VEP), 45

Web-based system, 177